D0102506

AMERICAN LITERATURE

FROM THE **1850s** TO **1945**

AMERICAN LITERATURE

FROM THE 1850s TO 1945

EDITED BY ADAM AUGUSTYN,
ASSISTANT MANAGER AND ASSISTANT EDITOR, LITERATURE

Educational Publishing

IN ASSOCIATION WITH

EDUCATIONAL SERVICES

Published in 2011 by Britannica Educational Publishing
(a trademark of Encyclopædia Britannica, Inc.)
in association with Rosen Educational Services, LLC
29 East 21st Street, New York, NY 10010.

First Edition

Britannica Educational Publishing
Michael I. Levy: Executive Editor
J.E. Luebering: Senior Manager
Marilyn L. Barton: Senior Coordinator, Production Control
Steven Bosco: Director, Editorial Technologies
Lisa S. Braucher: Senior Producer and Data Editor
Yvette Charboneau: Senior Copy Editor
Kathy Nakamura: Manager, Media Acquisition
Adam Augustyn: Assistant Manager and Assistant Editor, Literature

Rosen Educational Services
Jeanne Nagle: Senior Editor
Nelson Sá: Art Director
Cindy Reiman: Photography Director
Matthew Cauli: Designer, Cover Design
Introduction by Greg Roza

Library of Congress Cataloging-in-Publication Data

American literature from the 1850s to 1945 / edited by Adam Augustyn. — 1st ed.
    p. cm. — (The Britannica guide to world literature)
"In association with Britannica Educational Publishing, Rosen Educational Services."
Includes bibliographical references and index.
ISBN 978-1-61530-132-4 (library binding)
1. American literature—19th century—History and criticism. 2. American literature—
20th century—History and criticism. 3. American literature—19th century—
Bio-bibliography. 4. American literature—20th century—Bio-bibliography. I. Augustyn,
Adam, 1979–
PS201.A44 2011
810.9'004—dc22

                                                            2010006459

Manufactured in the United States of America

CONTENTS

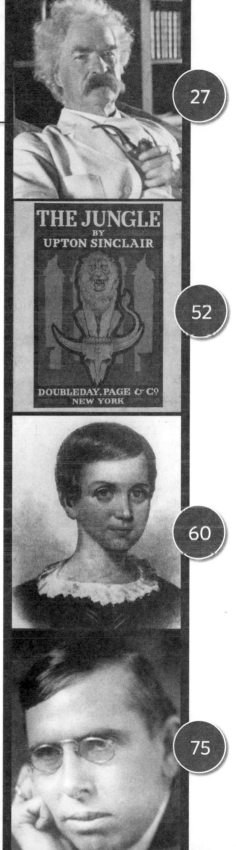

27

52

60

75

100

119

127

132

222

INTRODUCTION

At the end of the American Civil War in 1865, the United States embarked on an era of great change. Slavery had come to an end, and the economy had shifted from one based mainly on agriculture to one based on manufacturing. American literature also was changing, reflecting the country's transformation. This volume explores the works, writers, and movements that shaped the American literary canon from the end of the 19th century through the first half of the 20th.

One group of writers who gained popularity at this time were literary comedians who broke with the traditions of earlier American humorists, mixing poor grammar with learned literary allusions. Another group of writers, the local colourists, became known for writing stories that focused on the lives of people in various sections of the United States. Their aim was to create stories that were sometimes sentimental, sometimes humorous, and usually nostalgic for an earlier time. Among this group was William Sydney Porter—better known as O. Henry—who wrote short stories about the lives of ordinary people in New York City. His writings were frequently ironic and had surprise endings.

Samuel Langhorne Clemens eventually became the most memorable local colourist and comedic writer of the 19th century, as well as one of the most important writers in the American literary canon. Under the pen name Mark Twain, he started out writing humorous, lively newspaper articles and short stories, including his first true foray into fiction, "Jim Smiley and His Jumping Frog."

Ernest Hemingway, hard at work. Hemingway's spare style and simple dialogue were widely imitated, making him one of the most influential novelists of the 20th century. Kurt Hutton/Hulton Archive/Getty Images

The story was later renamed "The Celebrated Jumping Frog of Calaveras County," which became the eponymous anchor story for Twain's first published book of humorous sketches. For all the popularity of his comic works, Twain is perhaps best remembered for his adventure and travel stories (which nevertheless contained a good amount of humorous writing), such as *The Adventures of Tom Sawyer* (1876), *Life on the Mississippi* (1883), and *The Adventures of Huckleberry Finn* (1884). These stories draw vivid pictures of the life along the Mississippi River—a central character of his tales.

With the rise of industry, several American writers began featuring in their work the growing corruption they witnessed in big business and government. In 1880, Henry Adams (a descendant of presidents John Adams and John Quincy Adams) anonymously wrote *Democracy, an American Novel*. Adams's book reflected his growing lack of faith in the U.S. government. Adams is also known for his autobiography, *The Education of Henry Adams* (1918), in which he expresses his disillusionment with humankind and his fears of the modern, uncertain world. Another notable critic of the Gilded Age—the name given to the period of American materialistic excess in the decades following the Civil War—is Upton Sinclair, whose novel *The Jungle* (1906) denounced U.S. economics and politics, and suggested a shift to socialism. Sinclair was the most notable of a group of reform writers known as muckrakers, journalists who were openly critical of American policies on the pages of newspapers and magazines.

Among the U.S. poets who became popular in the years following the Civil War was Sidney Lanier. A musician as well as a writer, Lanier initially gained notoriety for his contrasting poems "Corn" (1875), which depicted agricultural conditions in the south, and "The Symphony" (1875), which addressed industrial conditions in the North. In addition to other poems and novels, Lanier also gave lectures on verse technique, early English poetry, and the English novel.

For most of her life, another beloved American poet of the age, Emily Dickinson, lived in seclusion in Amherst, Mass. Although she wrote nearly 1,800 poems during her lifetime, only 10 were published while she was alive. A unique lyric poet, Dickinson foreshadowed the modernist literary movement in her experiments with rhyme and grammar. She is also remembered for the many letters she wrote to friends and acquaintances, most of which feature her characteristic style.

Toward the end of the 19th century, a group of American writers gravitated toward the nascent naturalist movement, which was an extension of realism. Naturalists chose to present a "slice of life" without moral judgment, focusing instead on science-derived objectivity. Many naturalist writings offered a critical, often bleak view of American society. Among the earliest naturalists were William Dean Howells, Hamlin Garland, and Frank Norris. Stephen Crane's *The Red Badge of Courage* (1895), Jack London's *Call of the Wild* (1903), Edith Wharton's *Age of Innocence* (1920), and Theodore Dreiser's *An American Tragedy* (1925) are all prime examples of naturalist literature.

Although Henry James started out as a realist, his path diverged from those of the naturalists by placing an emphasis on the artist's perception of reality and how that perception is relayed to readers. Many critics laud James for ushering in the era of the modern American novel.

Among his most enduring works are *The Portrait of a Lady* (1881), *The Wings of the Dove* (1902), and *The Ambassadors* (1903). During the course of 51 years, he wrote 20 novels, 112 short stories, 12 plays, several volumes of travel and criticism, and a good amount of literary journalism. His recurring theme was innocent American society confronting the aristocratic culture of European society.

In the early portion of the 20th century, journalist and humorist H.L. Mencken had a powerful influence over American fiction. Mencken's satirical critiques helped release American writing from the rigid forms and morals of previous eras. His influence on American literature and journalism extended over the course of several decades. Mencken also helped pave the way for several American writers as he noted the importance of newcomers such as Theodore Dreiser and Sherwood Anderson.

By 1920, a new school of American fiction had risen to prominence, led by societal critics such as Sinclair Lewis and F. Scott Fitzgerald. Many American novels and short stories written during the 1920s included deep psychological musings on the profound disillusionment of the post–World War I generation. Perhaps the most notable example of the era is Fitzgerald's *The Great Gatsby* (1925), which explores the pain of failing to achieve the American Dream.

Around the same time, African American artists initiated a movement that became known as the Harlem Renaissance. Much of the literature produced by the writers of this movement addresses the difficulties and ironies of establishing a racial identity apart from the "Negro" stereotypes that had developed after years of slavery and inequality. Although some critics accused the artists of the Harlem Renaissance of eschewing African American values in order to be accepted by white society, others have said that it represented an open celebration of African American heritage. There's no doubt that the novels and poetry of this movement had a great and lasting affect on later African American literature. Noteworthy works from this movement include Richard Wright's novels *Native Son* (1940) and *Black Boy* (1945), Zora Neale Hurston's novel *Their Eyes Were Watching God* (1937), and the poetry and stories of Langston Hughes.

The works of Ernest Hemingway in the years after World War I were defined by a sense of disenchantment and skepticism. Hemingway was a member of the Lost Generation, a group of American writers living and writing in Paris in the postwar years (which also included E.E. Cummings, John Dos Passos, and F. Scott Fitzgerald) who were alienated from contemporary American values. Hemingway expressed these views in his earlier novels, such as *The Sun Also Rises* (1926) and *A Farewell to Arms* (1929). However, Hemingway later moved toward themes of social change through collective action. For example, he focused on the futility of war in *A Farewell to Arms*, while in *For Whom the Bell Tolls* (1940) conflict is treated as the catalyst for lasting and enduring friendships.

Whereas the power of Hemingway's writing comes from his spare style, William Faulkner's prose is known for its elaborate phrases and experimental structure. Faulkner's novels, which include *The Sound and the Fury* (1929), *As I Lay Dying* (1930), and *Absalom, Absalom!* (1936), combine modernist literary techniques such as stream-of-consciousness narratives from multiple characters' perspectives with rich historical tales of Southern families and communities. Key to his plots is the disintegration of preeminently successful Southern families in mythical Yoknapatawpha County, Miss.

Like Hemingway and Faulkner, John Steinbeck wrote fiction that was less enchanted with modern society than much of the literature of the time. Steinbeck's novels tell the stories of downtrodden outcasts and laborers, such as the migratory workers at the centre of his best-known work, *The Grapes of Wrath* (1939). An overarching message conveyed in many of Steinbeck's novels and short stories was the importance of collective action among the poor to keep the individual from being destroyed.

The early 20th century spirit of experimentation that infused the writings of Faulkner was even more prevalent in American drama and poetry of the time. After witnessing the thriving revolutionary theatre productions of Europe, American dramatists began the Little Theatre movement, which saw various groups of playwrights open their own small theatres to counter large commercial production companies. They worked with dramatic forms and production techniques theretofore untested in the United States.

Eugene O'Neill, a product of the Little Theatre movement, was the foremost American playwright of the era. His plays were both innovative and emotionally resonant. Between 1920 and 1943, O'Neill wrote 20 long plays — most notably *Mourning Becomes Electra* (1931), *The Iceman Cometh* (1939), and *Long Day's Journey into Night* (produced posthumously, 1956) — and a number of shorter ones. Turning from the poorly received melodramas of his early career, O'Neill refined his art and began producing plays with decidedly dark themes, contemporary tragedies that some critics believe rival those Shakespeare's works in terms of dramatic impact. O'Neill's works are deeply personal, drawing from conflicts in his own life. He was amply rewarded for his efforts, both critically and commercially. Winner of four Pulitzer Prizes for drama—and the first American playwright to receive a Nobel Prize for Literature (1936)—he became one of the most widely produced dramatists of all time.

Although O'Neill was the most famous playwright of the era, others had a hand in shaping the course of American drama as well. Playwright and screenwriter Lillian Hellman wrote powerful melodramas that explored the depths of evil. Two of her most famous plays, *The Children's Hour* (1934) and *The Little Foxes* (1939), are about the numerous ways in which people take advantage of others. Thornton Wilder won a Pulitzer Prize in 1928 for his novel *The Bridge of San Luis Rey*, but he is best remembered for the play *Our Town* (1938), an experimental production in which the actors play average small-town residents on a nearly bare stage.

Several talented writers experimented with new forms and styles to produce work that changed the landscape of American poetry, while others brought new life to old forms and techniques. The former group included distinguished figures such as Ezra Pound, a master of economic verse that aimed to reach the high standards of earlier masterpieces, and William Carlos Williams, whose formal experimentation was leavened with a strong romantic streak. The most noteworthy of the poets who worked within traditional poetic styles was Robert Frost, who is arguably the most commercially successful poet of the era.

No discussion of American literature in the early 20th century would be complete without mentioning T. S. Eliot. His poetic masterpiece, *The Waste Land* (1922), presents a dark and dismal perspective of the years following World War I, a time when many people had great difficulty comprehending the course of world affairs. Beyond having a deeply resonant theme, the poem also is noted for its exquisite phrasing and adventurous style. Eliot—like so many of the poets, novelists, and dramatists of the time—found that only by breaking free of established literary formats and themes could one attempt to find meaning and direction in the increasingly chaotic modern world.

FROM THE CIVIL WAR TO 1914

As with the Revolution and the election of Andrew Jackson before, the Civil War was a turning point in U.S. history and the beginning of new ways of living. Industry became increasingly important, factories rose and cities grew, and agrarian preeminence declined. The frontier, which before had always been an important factor in the economic scheme, moved steadily westward and, toward the end of the 19th century, vanished. The rise of modern America was accompanied, naturally, by important mutations in literature.

LITERARY COMEDIANS

As the country was thrust into the chaos of the Civil War, some authors dealt with the wartime horrors by turning to humour as an antidote. Although they continued to employ some devices of the older American humorists, the group of comic writers that rose to prominence at this time was different in important ways from the older group. Charles Farrar Browne, David Ross Locke, Charles Henry Smith, Henry Wheeler Shaw, and Edgar Wilson Nye wrote, respectively, as Artemus Ward, Petroleum V. (for Vesuvius) Nasby, Bill Arp, Josh Billings, and Bill Nye. Appealing to a national audience, these authors forsook the sectional characterizations of earlier humorists and assumed the roles of less individualized literary comedians. The nature of the humour thus shifted from character portrayal to verbal devices such as poor grammar, bad spelling, and slang, incongruously combined with Latinate words and learned allusions. Most that they wrote wore badly, but thousands of Americans in their time and some in later times found these authors vastly amusing, and they helped to pave the way for the more consequential comic writers of the late 19th and early 20th centuries.

Artemus Ward

(b. April 26, 1834, Waterford, Maine, U.S. — d. March 6, 1867, Southampton, Hampshire, Eng.)

Artemus Ward (the pseudonym of Charles Farrar Browne) was one of the most popular 19th-century American humorists. His lecture techniques exercised much influence on such humorists as Mark Twain.

Starting as a printer's apprentice, Browne went to Boston to work as a compositor for *The Carpet-Bag*, a humour magazine. In 1860, after several years as local editor for the Toledo (Ohio) *Commercial* and the Cleveland *Plain Dealer*, he became staff writer for *Vanity Fair* in New York.

While working on the *Plain Dealer*, Browne created the character Artemus Ward, the manager of an itinerant sideshow who "commented" on a variety of subjects in letters to the *Plain Dealer*, *Punch*, and *Vanity Fair*. The most obvious features of his humour are puns and gross misspellings. His works include *Artemus Ward: His Book* (1862); *Artemus Ward: His Travels* (1865); and *Artemus Ward in London* (1867).

In 1861 Browne turned to lecturing under the pseudonym Artemus Ward. Though his books were popular, it was his lecturing, delivered with deadpan expression, that brought him fame.

LOCAL COLOURISTS

The first group of fiction writers to become popular at this time — the local colourists — took over, to some extent, the task of portraying sectional groups that had been abandoned by writers of the new humour. Bret Harte, first of these writers to achieve wide success, admitted an indebtedness to prewar sectional humorists, as did some others; all showed resemblances to the earlier group. Within a brief period, books by pioneers in the movement appeared: Harriet Beecher Stowe's *Oldtown Folks* (1869) and *Sam Lawson's Oldtown Fireside Stories* (1871), delightful vignettes of New England; Harte's *Luck of Roaring Camp, and Other Sketches* (1870), humorous and sentimental tales of California mining camp life; and Edward Eggleston's *Hoosier Schoolmaster* (1871), a novel of the early days of the settlement of Indiana. Short stories (and a relatively small number of novels) in patterns set by these three continued to appear into the 20th century.

In time, practically every corner of the country had been portrayed in local-colour fiction. Additional writings were depictions of Louisiana Creoles by George W. Cable, New Orleans culture by Kate Chopin, Virginia blacks by Thomas Nelson Page, Georgia blacks by Joel Chandler Harris, Tennessee mountaineers by Mary Noailles Murfree (Charles Egbert Craddock), tight-lipped folk of New England by Sarah Orne Jewett and Mary E. Wilkins Freeman, New York City life by Henry Cuyler Bunner and William Sydney Porter ("O. Henry"), and life on the Mississippi River by the most prominent local colourist of them all, Mark Twain. The avowed aim of some of these writers was to portray realistically the lives of various sections and thus to promote understanding in a united nation. The stories as a rule were only partially realistic, however, since the authors tended nostalgically to revisit the past instead of portraying their own time, winnow out less glamorous aspects of life, or develop their stories with sentiment or humour. Touched by romance though they were, these fictional works were transitional to realism, for they portrayed common folk sympathetically, and concerned themselves with dialect and mores. Some, at least, avoided older sentimental or romantic formulas.

Kate Chopin
(b. Feb. 8, 1851, St. Louis, Mo., U.S.—d. Aug. 22, 1904, St. Louis)

Kate Chopin was an American novelist and short-story writer known as an interpreter of New Orleans culture. Chopin's work has been categorized within the local colour genre. There was a revival of interest in Chopin in the late 20th century because her concerns about the freedom of women foreshadowed later feminist literary themes.

Born to a prominent St. Louis family, Katherine O'Flaherty read widely as a girl. In June 1870 she married Oscar Chopin, with whom she lived in his native New Orleans, La., and later on a plantation near Cloutiersville, La., until his death in 1882. After he died she began to write about the Creole and Cajun people she had observed in the South. Her first novel, *At Fault* (1890), was undistinguished, but she was later acclaimed for her finely crafted short stories, of which she wrote more than 100. Two of these stories, "Désirée's Baby" and "Madame Celestin's Divorce," continue to be widely anthologized.

In 1899 Chopin published *The Awakening*, a realistic novel about the sexual and artistic awakening of a young wife and mother who abandons her family and eventually commits suicide. This work was roundly condemned in its time because of its sexual frankness and its portrayal of an interracial marriage and went out of print for more than

50 years. When it was rediscovered in the 1950s, critics marveled at the beauty of its writing and its modern sensibility.

Chopin's stories were collected in *Bayou Folk* (1894) and *A Night in Acadie* (1897). *The Complete Works of Kate Chopin*, edited by Per Seyersted, appeared in 1969.

WILLIAM SYDNEY PORTER

(b. Sept. 11, 1862, Greensboro, N.C., U.S.—d. June 5, 1910, New York, N.Y.)

The American short-story writer William Sydney Porter, writing under the pseudonym O. Henry, was notable for his tales that romanticized the commonplace, in particular the life of ordinary people in New York City. His stories expressed the effect of coincidence on character through humour, grim or ironic, and often had surprise endings, a device that became identified with his name and cost him critical favour when its vogue had passed.

Porter attended a school taught by his aunt, then clerked in his uncle's drugstore. In 1882 he went to Texas, where he worked on a ranch, in a general land office, and later as teller in the First National Bank in Austin. He began writing sketches at about the time of his marriage to Athol Estes in 1887, and in 1894 he started a humorous weekly, *The Rolling Stone*. When that venture failed, Porter joined the *Houston Post* as a reporter, columnist, and occasional cartoonist.

In February 1896 he was indicted for embezzlement of bank funds. Friends aided his flight to Honduras. News of his wife's fatal illness, however, took him back to Austin, and lenient authorities did not press his case until after her death. When convicted, Porter received the lightest sentence possible, and in 1898 he entered the penitentiary at Columbus, Ohio; his sentence was shortened to three years and three months for good behaviour. As night druggist in the prison hospital, he could write to earn money for support of his daughter Margaret. His stories of adventure in the southwest U.S. and Central America were immediately popular with magazine readers, and when he emerged from prison W.S. Porter had become O. Henry.

In 1902 O. Henry arrived in New York—his "Bagdad on the Subway." From December 1903 to January 1906 he produced a story a week for the New York *World*, writing also for magazines. His first book, *Cabbages and Kings* (1904), depicted fantastic characters against exotic Honduran backgrounds. Both *The Four Million* (1906) and *The Trimmed Lamp* (1907) explored the lives of the multitude of New York in their daily routines and searchings for romance and adventure. *Heart of the West* (1907) presented accurate and fascinating tales of the Texas range.

Then in rapid succession came *The Voice of the City* (1908), *The Gentle Grafter* (1908), *Roads of Destiny* (1909), *Options* (1909), *Strictly Business* (1910), and *Whirligigs* (1910). *Whirligigs* contains perhaps Porter's funniest story, "The Ransom of Red Chief."

Despite his popularity, O. Henry's final years were marred by ill health, a desperate financial struggle, and alcoholism. A second marriage in 1907 was unhappy. After his death three more collected volumes appeared: *Sixes and Sevens* (1911), *Rolling Stones* (1912), and *Waifs and Strays* (1917). Later seven fugitive stories and poems, *O. Henryana* (1920), *Letters to Lithopolis* (1922), and two collections of his early work on the *Houston Post, Postscripts* (1923) and *O. Henry Encore* (1939), were published. Foreign translations and adaptations for other art forms, including films and television, attest his universal application and appeal.

MARK TWAIN

(b. Nov. 30, 1835, Florida, Mo., U.S.—d. April 21, 1910, Redding, Conn.)

The American humorist, journalist, lecturer, and novelist Mark Twain acquired international fame for his travel narratives, especially *The Innocents Abroad* (1869), *Roughing It* (1872), and *Life on the Mississippi* (1883), and for his adventure stories of boyhood, especially *The Adventures of Tom Sawyer* (1876) and *Adventures of Huckleberry Finn* (1885). A gifted raconteur, distinctive humorist, and irascible moralist, he transcended the apparent limitations of his origins to become a popular public figure and one of America's best and most beloved writers.

Mark Twain. Library of Congress, Washington, D.C. LC-USZ62-112728

APPRENTICESHIPS

Born Samuel Langhorne Clemens, Twain became a printers apprentice as a boy. That experience exposed him to the prewar sectional humorists. Having acquired a profession by age 17, Clemens left his hometown of Hannibal, Mo., in 1853 with some degree of self-sufficiency. For almost two decades he would be an itinerant labourer, trying many occupations. It was not until he was 37, he once remarked, that he woke up to discover he had become a "literary person."

In February 1863 Clemens covered the legislative session in Carson City and wrote three letters for the *Enterprise*. He signed them "Mark Twain." Apparently the mistranscription of a telegram misled Clemens to believe that the pilot Isaiah Sellers had died and that his cognomen was up for grabs. Clemens seized it. It would be several years before this pen name would acquire the firmness of a full-fledged literary persona, however. In the meantime, he was discovering by degrees what it meant to be a "literary person."

Already he was acquiring a reputation outside the territory. Some of his articles and sketches had appeared in New York papers, and he became the Nevada correspondent for the San Francisco *Morning Call*. In 1864, after challenging the editor of a rival newspaper to a duel and then fearing the legal consequences for this indiscretion, he left Virginia City for San Francisco and became a full-time reporter for the *Call*. Finding that work tiresome, he began contributing to the *Golden Era* and the new literary magazine the *Californian*, edited by Bret Harte. After he published an article expressing his fiery indignation at police corruption in San Francisco, and after a man with whom he associated was arrested in a brawl, Clemens decided it prudent to leave the city for a time.

He went to the Tuolumne foothills to do some mining. It was there that he heard the story of a jumping frog. The story was widely known, but it was new to Clemens, and he took notes for a literary representation of the tale.

When the humorist Artemus Ward invited him to contribute something for a book of humorous sketches,
Clemens decided to write up the story. "Jim Smiley and
His Jumping Frog" arrived too late to be included in the
volume, but it was published in the New York *Saturday
Press* in November 1865 and was subsequently reprinted
throughout the country. "Mark Twain" had acquired sudden celebrity, and Sam Clemens was following in his wake.

LITERARY MATURITY

The next few years were important for Clemens. After he
had finished writing the jumping-frog story but before it
was published, he declared in a letter to his brother Orion
that he had a "'call' to literature of a low order—i.e. humorous. It is nothing to be proud of," he continued, "but it is
my strongest suit."

However much he might deprecate his calling, it
appears that he was committed to making a professional
career for himself. He continued to write for newspapers,
traveling to Hawaii for the Sacramento *Union* and also
writing for New York newspapers, but he apparently
wanted to become something more than a journalist. He
went on his first lecture tour, speaking mostly on the
Sandwich Islands (Hawaii) in 1866. It was a success, and
for the rest of his life, though he found touring grueling,
he knew he could take to the lecture platform when he
needed money.

Meanwhile, he tried, unsuccessfully, to publish a book
made up of his letters from Hawaii. His first book was in
fact *The Celebrated Jumping Frog of Calaveras County and
Other Sketches* (1867), but it did not sell well. That same
year, he moved to New York City, serving as the traveling
correspondent for the San Francisco *Alta California* and
for New York newspapers. He had ambitions to enlarge
his reputation and his audience, and the announcement of

a transatlantic excursion to Europe and the Holy Land provided him with just such an opportunity. The *Alta* paid the substantial fare in exchange for some 50 letters he would write concerning the trip. Eventually his account of the voyage was published as *The Innocents Abroad* (1869). It was a great success.

The trip abroad was fortuitous in another way. He met on the boat a young man named Charlie Langdon, who invited Clemens to dine with his family in New York and introduced him to his sister Olivia; the writer fell in love with her. Clemens's courtship of Olivia Langdon, the daughter of a prosperous businessman from Elmira, N.Y., was an ardent one, conducted mostly through correspondence. They were married in February 1870. With financial assistance from Olivia's father, Clemens bought a one-third interest in the *Express* of Buffalo, N.Y., and began writing a column for a New York City magazine, the *Galaxy*. A son, Langdon, was born in November 1870, but the boy was frail and would die of diphtheria less than two years later.

Clemens came to dislike Buffalo and hoped that he and his family might move to the Nook Farm area of Hartford, Conn. In the meantime, he worked hard on a book about his experiences in the West. *Roughing It* was published in February 1872 and sold well. The next month, Olivia Susan (Susy) Clemens was born in Elmira. Later that year, Clemens traveled to England. Upon his return, he began work with his friend Charles Dudley Warner on a satirical novel about political and financial corruption in the United States. *The Gilded Age* (1873) was remarkably well received, and a play based on the most amusing character from the novel, Colonel Sellers, also became quite popular.

The Gilded Age was Twain's first attempt at a novel, and the experience was apparently congenial enough for

Mark Twain, lithograph from Puck, *1885.* Library of Congress, Washington, D.C. LC-USZC4-4294

him to begin writing *Tom Sawyer*, along with his reminiscences about his days as a riverboat pilot. He also published "A True Story," a moving dialect sketch told by a former slave, in the prestigious *Atlantic Monthly* in 1874. A second daughter, Clara, was born in June, and the Clemenses moved into their still-unfinished house in Nook Farm later the same year, counting among their neighbours Warner and the writer Harriet Beecher Stowe. *Old Times on the Mississippi* appeared in the *Atlantic* in installments in 1875.

The obscure journalist from the wilds of California and Nevada had arrived. He had settled down in a comfortable house with his family. He was known worldwide, his books sold well, and he was a popular favourite on the lecture tour. His fortunes had steadily improved over the years. In the process, the journalistic and satirical temperament of the writer had, at times, become retrospective. *Old Times*, which would later become a portion of *Life on the Mississippi*, described comically, but a bit ruefully too, a way of life that would never return. The highly episodic narrative of *Tom Sawyer*, which recounts the mischievous adventures of a boy growing up along the Mississippi River, was coloured by a nostalgia for childhood and simplicity that would permit Twain to characterize the novel as a "hymn" to childhood. The continuing popularity of *Tom Sawyer* (it sold well from its first publication, in 1876, and has never gone out of print) indicates that Twain could write a novel that appealed to young and old readers alike. The antics and high adventure of Tom Sawyer and his comrades—including pranks in church and at school, the comic courtship of Becky Thatcher, a murder mystery, and a thrilling escape from a cave—continue to delight children, while the book's comedy, narrated by someone who vividly recalls what it was to be a child, amuses adults with similar memories.

In the summer of 1876, while staying with his in-laws Susan and Theodore Crane on Quarry Farm overlooking Elmira, Clemens began writing what he called in a letter to his friend William Dean Howells "Huck Finn's Autobiography." Huck had appeared as a character in *Tom Sawyer*, and Clemens decided that the untutored boy had his own story to tell. He soon discovered that it had to be told in Huck's own vernacular voice. *Huckleberry Finn* was written in fits and starts over an extended period and would not be published until 1885. During that interval, Twain often turned his attention to other projects, only to return again and again to the novel's manuscript.

Twain believed he had humiliated himself before Boston's literary worthies when he delivered one of many speeches at a dinner commemorating the 70th birthday of poet and abolitionist John Greenleaf Whittier. Twain's contribution to the occasion fell flat (perhaps because of a failure of delivery or the contents of the speech itself), and some believed he had insulted three literary icons in particular: Henry Wadsworth Longfellow, Ralph Waldo Emerson, and Oliver Wendell Holmes. The embarrassing experience may have in part prompted his removal to Europe for nearly two years. He published *A Tramp Abroad* (1880), about his travels with his friend Joseph Twichell in the Black Forest and the Swiss Alps, and *The Prince and the Pauper* (1881), a fanciful tale set in 16th-century England and written for "young people of all ages." In 1882 he traveled up the Mississippi with Horace Bixby, taking notes for the book that became *Life on the Mississippi* (1883).

All the while, he continued to make often ill-advised investments, the most disastrous of which was the continued financial support of an inventor, James W. Paige, who was perfecting an automatic typesetting machine. In 1884 Clemens founded his own publishing company, bearing the name of his nephew and business agent, Charles L.

Webster, and embarked on a four-month lecture tour with fellow author George W. Cable, both to raise money for the company and to promote the sales of *Huckleberry Finn*. Not long after that, Clemens began the first of several Tom-and-Huck sequels. None of them would rival *Huckleberry Finn*.

For a time, Clemens's prospects seemed rosy. After working closely with Ulysses S. Grant, he watched as his company's publication of the former U.S. president's memoirs in 1885–86 became an overwhelming success. Clemens believed a forthcoming biography of Pope Leo XIII would do even better. The prototype for the Paige typesetter also seemed to be working splendidly. It was in a generally sanguine mood that he began to write *A Connecticut Yankee in King Arthur's Court*, about the exploits of a practical and democratic factory superintendent who is magically transported to Camelot and attempts to transform the kingdom according to 19th-century republican values and modern technology. So confident was he about prospects for the typesetter that Clemens predicted this novel would be his "swan-song" to literature and that he would live comfortably off the profits of his investment.

Things did not go according to plan, however. His publishing company was floundering, and cash flow problems meant he was drawing on his royalties to provide capital for the business. Clemens was suffering from rheumatism in his right arm, but he continued to write for magazines out of necessity. Still, he was getting deeper and deeper in debt, and by 1891 he had ceased his monthly payments to support work on the Paige typesetter, effectively giving up on an investment that over the years had cost him some $200,000 or more. He closed his beloved house in Hartford, and the family moved to Europe, where they might live more cheaply and, perhaps, where his wife, who had always been frail, might improve her health. Debts continued to mount, and the financial panic of 1893 made it difficult to borrow money. Luckily, he was befriended by a Standard Oil executive, Henry Huttleston Rogers, who undertook to put Clemens's financial house in order. Clemens assigned his property, including his copyrights, to Olivia, announced the failure of his publishing house, and declared personal bankruptcy. In 1894, approaching his 60th year, Samuel Clemens was forced to repair his fortunes and to remake his career.

LATER YEARS

Late in 1894 *The Tragedy of Pudd'nhead Wilson and the Comedy of Those Extraordinary Twins* was published. Set in the antebellum South, *Pudd'nhead Wilson* concerns the fates of transposed babies, one white and the other black, and is a fascinating, if ambiguous, exploration of the social and legal construction of race. It also reflects Twain's thoughts on determinism, a subject that would increasingly occupy his thoughts for the remainder of his life. One of the maxims from that novel jocularly expresses his point of view: "Training is everything. The peach was once a bitter almond; cauliflower is nothing but cabbage with a college education." Clearly, despite his reversal of fortunes, Twain had not lost his sense of humour. But he was frustrated too—frustrated by financial difficulties but also by the public's perception of him as a funnyman and nothing more. The persona of Mark Twain had become something of a curse for Samuel Clemens.

Clemens published his next novel, *Personal Recollections of Joan of Arc* (serialized 1895–96), anonymously in hopes that the public might take it more seriously than a book bearing the Mark Twain name. The strategy did not work, for it soon became generally known that he was the author; when the novel was first published in book form, in 1896, his name appeared on the volume's spine but not on its title page. However, in later years he would publish some works anonymously, and still others he declared could not be published until long after his death, on the largely erroneous assumption that his true views would scandalize the public. Clemens's sense of wounded pride was necessarily compromised by his indebtedness, and he embarked on a lecture tour in July 1895 that would take him across North America to Vancouver, B.C., Can., and from there around the world. He gave lectures in Australia, New Zealand, India, South Africa, and points in-between, arriving in England a little more than a year afterward. Clemens was in London when he was notified of the death of his daughter Susy, of spinal meningitis. A pall settled over the Clemens household; they would not celebrate birthdays or holidays for the next several years.

As an antidote to his grief as much as anything else, Clemens threw himself into work. He wrote a great deal he did not intend to publish during those years, but he did publish *Following the Equator* (1897), a relatively serious account of his world lecture tour. By 1898 the revenue generated from the tour and the subsequent book, along with Henry Huttleston Rogers's shrewd investments of his money, had allowed Clemens to pay his creditors in full. Rogers was shrewd as well in the way he publicized and redeemed the reputation of "Mark Twain" as a man of impeccable moral character. Palpable tokens of public approbation are the three honorary degrees conferred on Clemens in his last years—from Yale University in 1901, from the University of Missouri in 1902, and, the one he most coveted, from Oxford University in 1907. When he traveled to Missouri to receive his honorary Doctor of Laws, he visited old friends in Hannibal along the way. He knew that it would be his last visit to his hometown.

Clemens had acquired the esteem and moral authority he had yearned for only a few years before, and the writer

Mark Twain, c. *1907.* Library of Congress, Washington, D.C.
LC-USZ62-117475

made good use of his reinvigorated position. He began writing "The Man That Corrupted Hadleyburg" (1899), a devastating satire of venality in small-town America, and the first of three manuscript versions of *The Mysterious Stranger*. (None of the manuscripts was ever completed, and they were posthumously combined and published in 1916.) He also started *What Is Man?* (published anonymously in 1906), a dialogue in which a wise "Old Man" converts a resistant "Young Man" to a brand of philosophical determinism. He began to dictate his autobiography, which he would continue to do until a few months before he died. Some of Twain's best work during his late years was not fiction but polemical essays in which his earnestness was not in doubt: an essay against anti-Semitism, "Concerning the Jews" (1899); a denunciation of imperialism, "To the Man Sitting in Darkness" (1901); an essay on lynching, "The United States of Lyncherdom" (posthumously published in 1923); and a pamphlet on the brutal and exploitative Belgian rule in the Congo, *King Leopold's Soliloquy* (1905).

ASSESSMENT

As a humorist and as a moralist, Twain worked best in short pieces. *Roughing It* is a rollicking account of his adventures in the American West, but it is also seasoned with such exquisite yarns as "Buck Fanshaw's Funeral" and "The Story of the Old Ram"; *A Tramp Abroad* is for many readers a disappointment, but it does contain the nearly perfect "Jim Baker's Blue-Jay Yarn." In "A True Story," told in an African American dialect, Twain transformed the resources of the typically American humorous story into something serious and profoundly moving. "The Man That Corrupted Hadleyburg" is relentless social satire; it is also the most formally controlled piece Twain ever wrote. The originality of the longer works is often to be found more in their conception than in their sustained execution. *The Innocents Abroad* is perhaps the funniest of all of Twain's books, but it also redefined the genre of the travel narrative by attempting to suggest to the reader, as Twain wrote, "how *he* would be likely to see Europe and the East if he looked at them with his own eyes." Similarly, in *Tom Sawyer*, he treated childhood not as the achievement of obedience to adult authority but as a period of mischief-making fun and good-natured affection.

Like Miguel de Cervantes's *Don Quixote*, which Twain much admired, *Huckleberry Finn* made changes in the picaresque novel that are of permanent interest. All of the Tom-and-Huck narratives engage in broad comedy and pointed satire, and they show that Twain had not lost his ability to speak in Huck's voice. What distinguishes *Huckleberry Finn* from the others is the moral dilemma Huck faces in aiding the runaway slave Jim while at the same time escaping from the unwanted influences of so-called civilization. Through Huck, the novel's narrator, Twain was able to address the shameful legacy of chattel slavery prior to the Civil War and the persistent racial discrimination and violence after. That he did so in the voice and consciousness of a 14-year-old boy, a character who shows the signs of having been trained to accept the cruel and indifferent attitudes of a slaveholding culture, gives the novel its affecting power, which can elicit genuine sympathies in readers but can also generate controversy and debate and can affront those who find the book patronizing toward African Americans, if not perhaps much worse. If *Huckleberry Finn* is a great book of American literature, its greatness may lie in its continuing ability to touch a nerve in the American national consciousness that is still raw and troubling.

Twain was not the first Anglo-American to treat the problems of race and racism in all their complexity, but, along with that of Herman Melville, his treatment remains of vital interest more than a hundred years later. His ability to swiftly and convincingly create a variety of fictional characters rivals that of Charles Dickens. And his mastery of spoken language, of slang and argot and dialect, gave these figures a voice. Twain's democratic sympathies and his steadfast refusal to condescend to the lowliest of his creations give the whole of his literary production a point of view that is far more expansive, interesting, and challenging than his somewhat crusty philosophical speculations. Howells, who had known most of the important American literary figures of the 19th century and thought them to be more or less like one another, believed that Twain was unique. Twain will always be remembered first and foremost as a humorist, but he was a great deal more—a public moralist, popular entertainer, political philosopher, travel writer, and novelist. Perhaps it is too much to claim, as some have, that Twain invented the American point of view in fiction, but that such a notion might be entertained indicates that his place in American literary culture is secure.

OTHER STANDOUT WRITERS OF THE PERIOD

Not all authors of the Civil War era fit easily into the categories of literary comedians or local colourists. Two of the most notable of these writers were Louisa May Alcott, who produced bestselling semiautobiographical works about domestic life, and Horatio Alger, whose characteristic tales of people building themselves up from nothing have resulted in his name being a byword for rags-to-riches stories to this day.

LOUISA MAY ALCOTT

(b. Nov. 29, 1832, Germantown, Pa., U.S.—d. March 6, 1888, Boston, Mass.)

Louisa May Alcott, portrait by George Healy; in the Louisa May Alcott Memorial Association collection, Concord, Massachusetts. Louisa May Alcott Memorial Association

Louisa May Alcott was an American author known for her children's books, especially the classic *Little Women*.

A daughter of the transcendentalist Bronson Alcott, Louisa spent most of her life in Boston and Concord, Mass., where she grew up in the company of Ralph Waldo Emerson, Theodore Parker, and Henry David Thoreau. Her education was largely under the direction of her father, for a time at his innovative Temple School in Boston and, later, at home. Alcott realized early that her father was too impractical to provide for his wife and four daughters; after the failure of Fruitlands, a utopian community that he had founded, Louisa Alcott's lifelong concern for the welfare of her family began. She taught briefly, worked as a domestic, and finally began to write.

Alcott produced potboilers at first and many of her stories—notably those signed "A.M. Barnard"—were lurid and violent tales. The latter works are unusual in their depictions of women as strong, self-reliant, and imaginative. She volunteered as a nurse after the American Civil War began, but she contracted typhoid from unsanitary hospital conditions and was sent home. She was never completely well again. The publication of her letters in book form, *Hospital Sketches* (1863), brought her the first taste of fame.

Alcott's stories began to appear in *The Atlantic Monthly*, and, because family needs were pressing, she wrote the autobiographical *Little Women* (1868–69), which was an immediate success. Based on her recollections of her own childhood, *Little Women* describes the domestic adventures of a New England family of modest means but optimistic outlook. The book traces the differing personalities and fortunes of four sisters as they emerge from childhood and encounter the vicissitudes of employment, society, and marriage. *Little Women* created a realistic but wholesome picture of family life with which younger readers could easily identify. In 1869 Alcott was able to write in her journal: "Paid up all the debts . . . thank the Lord!" She followed *Little Women*'s success with further domestic narratives drawn from her early experiences: *An Old-Fashioned Girl* (1870); *Aunt Jo's Scrap Bag*, 6 vol. (1872–82); *Little Men* (1871); *Eight Cousins* (1875); *Rose in Bloom* (1876); and *Jo's Boys* (1886).

Except for a European tour in 1870 and a few briefer trips to New York, she spent the last two decades of her life in Boston and Concord, caring for her mother, who died in 1877 after a lengthy illness, and her increasingly helpless father. Late in life she adopted her namesake, Louisa May Nieriker, daughter of her late sister, May. Her own health, never robust, also declined, and she died in Boston two days after her father's death.

Alcott's books for younger readers have remained steadfastly popular, and the republication of some of her lesser-known works late in the 20th century aroused renewed critical interest in her adult fiction. *A Modern Mephistopheles,* which was published pseudonymously in 1877 and republished in 1987, is a Gothic novel about a failed poet who makes a Faustian bargain with his tempter. *Work: A Story of Experience* (1873), based on Alcott's own struggles, tells the story of a poor girl trying to support herself by a succession of menial jobs. The Gothic tales and thrillers that Alcott published pseudonymously between 1863 and 1869 were collected and republished as *Behind a Mask* (1975) and *Plots and Counterplots* (1976). An unpublished Gothic novel written in 1866, *A Long Fatal Love Chase,* was published in 1995.

HORATIO ALGER

(b. Jan. 13, 1832, Chelsea, Mass., U.S.—d. July 18, 1899, Natick, Mass.),

One of the most popular American authors in the last 30 years of the 19th century, Horatio Alger was perhaps the most socially influential American writer of his generation.

Alger was the son of a Unitarian minister, Horatio Alger, Sr., who tutored him in reading from the age of six. The young Alger showed an interest in writing, and at Harvard University he distinguished himself in the classics and graduated in 1852 with Phi Beta Kappa honours. After leaving Harvard, Alger worked as a schoolteacher and contributed to magazines. In 1857 he enrolled in the Harvard Divinity School, from which he took his degree in 1860. He then took a seven-month tour of Europe and returned to the United States shortly after the outbreak of the American Civil War. During the war he was rejected for army service.

Alger was ordained in 1864, and he accepted the pulpit of a church in Brewster, Mass., but he was forced to leave in 1866 following allegations of sexual activities with local boys. In that year he moved to New York City, and, with the publication and sensational success of *Ragged Dick; or, Street Life in New York with the Bootblacks* (serialized in 1867, published in book form in 1868), the story of a poor shoe-shine boy who rises to wealth, Alger found his lifelong theme. In the more than 100 books that he would write over 30 years, Alger followed the rags-to-riches formula that he had hit upon in his first book.

The success of *Ragged Dick* led Alger to actively support charitable institutions for the support of foundlings and runaway boys. It was in this atmosphere that Alger wrote stories of boys who rose from poverty to wealth and fame, stories that were to make him famous and contribute the "Alger hero" to the American language. In a steady succession of books that are almost alike except for the names of their characters, he preached that by honesty, cheerful perseverance, and hard work, the poor but virtuous lad would have his just reward—though the reward was almost always precipitated by a stroke of good luck. Alger's novels had enormous popular appeal at a time when great personal fortunes were being made and seemingly unbounded opportunities for advancement existed in the United

Horatio Alger. Library of Congress, Washington, D.C.

States' burgeoning industrial cities. Alger's most popular books were the Ragged Dick, Luck and Pluck, and Tattered Tom series. His books sold over 20 million copies, even though their plots, characterizations, and dialogue were consistently and even outrageously bad.

By the mid-1890s his health was waning, and Alger settled in Natick, Mass., with his sister Olive and her husband. He died there a few years later.

CRITICS OF THE GILDED AGE

Writers of many types of works contributed to a great body of literature that flourished between the Civil War and 1914—literature of social revolt. The period itself drew its name from Twain and Warner's novel *The Gilded Age*. Novels attacked the growing power of business and the growing corruption of government, and some novelists outlined utopias. Political corruption and inefficiency figured in Henry Adams's novel *Democracy* (1880). Edward Bellamy's *Looking Backward* (1888) was both an indictment of the capitalistic system and an imaginative picturing of a utopia achieved by a collectivist society in the year 2000. Howells's *Traveler from Altruria* (1894) pleaded for an equalitarian state in which the government regimented men's lives.

Two poets embodied criticisms in songs. Edwin Markham's "Man with the Hoe" (1899) was a protest against the exploitation of labour and vaguely threatened revolution; it immediately stimulated nationwide interest. A year later William Vaughn Moody's "Ode in Time of Hesitation" denounced growing U.S. imperialism as a desertion of earlier principles; his "On a Soldier Fallen in the Philippines" (1901) developed the same theme even more effectively.

With the rise of journalistic magazines, a group of journalists became notable as critics of America—the group dubbed "the muckrakers" by Theodore Roosevelt. Ida M. Tarbell's *The History of the Standard Oil Company* (1904) and Lincoln Steffens's *The Shame of the Cities* (1904) were typical contributions by two members of a large group of journalistic crusaders.

HENRY ADAMS

One of the most devastating and most literate attacks on modern life was an autobiography of a scion of an ancient New England family, the Adamses. Educated at Harvard and abroad, Henry Adams was a great teacher and historian (in noteworthy works such as *History of the United States* [1889–91] and *Mont-Saint-Michel and Chartres* [1904]). *The Education of Henry Adams* (printed privately 1906; published 1918), however, complained that a lifelong hunt for some sort of order in the world, some sort of faith for man, left him completely baffled. The quiet, urbane style served well to underline, in an ironic way, the message of this pessimistic book.

Adams was born in 1838, the product of Boston's Brahmin class, a cultured elite that traced its lineage to Puritan New England. He was the great-grandson of John Adams and the grandson of John Quincy Adams, both presidents of the United States. The Adams family tradition of leadership was carried on by his father, Charles Francis Adams (1807–86), a diplomat, historian, and congressman. His younger brother, Brooks (1848–1927), was also a historian; his older brother, Charles Francis, Jr. (1835–1915), was an author and railroad executive. Through his mother, Abigail Brown Brooks, Adams was related to one of the most distinguished and wealthiest families in Boston. Tradition ingrained a deep sense of morality in Adams. He never escaped his heritage and often spoke of himself as a child of the 17th and 18th centuries who was forced to come to terms with the new world of the 20th century.

Adams was graduated from Harvard in 1858 and, in typical patrician fashion, embarked upon a grand tour of Europe in search of amusement and a vocation. Anticipating a career as an attorney, he spent the winter of 1859 attending lectures in civil law at the University of Berlin. With the outbreak of the U.S. Civil War in 1861, Pres. Abraham Lincoln appointed Adams's father minister to England. Henry, age 23, accompanied him to London, acting as his private secretary until 1868.

Returning to the United States, Adams travelled to Washington, D.C., as a newspaper correspondent for *The Nation* and other leading journals. He plunged into the capital's social and political life, anxious to begin the reconstruction of a nation shattered by war. He called for civil service reform and retention of the silver standard. Adams wrote numerous essays exposing political corruption and warning against the growing power of economic monopolies, particularly railroads. These articles were published in *Chapters of Erie and Other Essays* (1871). The mediocrity of the nation's "statesmen" constantly irritated him. Adams liked to repeat Pres. Ulysses S. Grant's remark that Venice would be a fine city if it were drained.

Adams continued his reformist activities as editor of the *North American Review* (1870–76). Moreover, he participated in the Liberal Republican movement. This group of insurgents, repelled by partisanship and the scandals of the Grant administration, bolted the Republican Party in 1872 and nominated the Democrat Horace Greeley for president. Their crusade soon foundered. Adams grew disillusioned with a world he characterized as devoid of principle. He was disgusted with demagogic politicians and a society in which all became "servant[s] of the powerhouse." Americans, he wrote, "had no time for thought;

they saw, and could see, nothing beyond their day's work; their attitude to the universe outside them was that of the deep-sea fish." His anonymously published novel *Democracy, an American Novel* (1880) reflected his loss of faith. The heroine, Madeleine Lee, like Adams himself, becomes an intimate of Washington's political circles. As confidante of a Midwestern senator, Madeleine is introduced to the democratic process. She meets the president and other figures who are equally vacuous. After her contact with the power brokers, Madeleine concluded: "Democracy has shaken my nerves to pieces."

In 1870 Charles W. Eliot, president of Harvard College, appointed Adams professor of medieval history. He was the first American to employ the seminar method in teaching history. In 1877 he resigned to edit the papers of Thomas Jefferson's treasury secretary, Albert Gallatin. Pursuing his interest in U.S. history, Adams completed two biographies, *The Life of Albert Gallatin* (1879) and *John Randolph* (1882). He continued to delve into the nation's early national period, hoping to understand the nature of an evolving American democracy. This study culminated in his nine-volume *History of the United States of America* during the administrations of Jefferson and Madison, a scholarly work that received immediate acclaim after its publication (1889–91). In this work he explored the dilemma of governing an egalitarian society in a political world in which the predominant tendency was to aggrandize power. In 1884 Adams wrote another novel, *Esther.* Published under a pseudonym, *Esther* dealt with the relationship between religion and modern science, a theme that engaged Adams throughout his life.

Adams was stunned when, in 1885, his wife of 13 years, Marian Hooper, committed suicide. Distraught, he arranged for the sculpture of a mysterious, cloaked woman to be placed upon her grave. The union had produced no children, and Adams never remarried. After his wife's death, Adams began a period of restless wandering. He travelled the globe from the South Sea islands to the Middle East. Gradually the circuit narrowed to winters in Washington and summers in Paris.

Though Adams referred to his existence during this period as that of a "cave-dweller," his life was quite the opposite. From the 1870s until his last years, intellectuals gravitated to his home to discuss art, science, politics, and literature. Among them were the British diplomat Sir Cecil Arthur Spring-Rice, the architect Henry Hobson Richardson, and Sen. Henry Cabot Lodge. His closest friends were the geologist Clarence King and the diplomat John Hay. Adams and King were inseparable. Their letters remain a rich source of information on everything from gossip to the most current trends of thought.

While in France, Adams pushed further into the recesses of history in search of "a fixed point . . . from which he might measure motion down to his own time." That point became medieval Christendom in the 13th century. In *Mont-Saint-Michel and Chartres* (printed privately, 1904; published, 1913) he described the medieval world view as reflected in its cathedrals. These buildings, he believed, expressed "an emotion, the deepest man ever felt—the struggle of his own littleness to grasp the infinite." Adams' attraction to the Middle Ages lay in the era's ideological unity; a coherence expressed in Catholicism and symbolized by the Virgin Mary.

The Education of Henry Adams was a companion volume to *Chartres*. The *Education* remains Adams's best known work and one of the most distinguished of all autobiographies. In contrast to *Chartres,* the *Education* centred upon the 20th-century universe of multiplicity, particularly the exploding world of science and technology. In opposition to the medieval Virgin, Adams saw a new godhead—the dynamo—symbol of modern history's anarchic energies. The *Education* recorded his failure to understand the centrifugal forces of contemporary life. The book traced Adams's confrontations with reality as he moved from the custom-bound world of his birth into the modern, existential universe in which certainties had vanished.

Neither history nor education provided an answer for Henry Adams. Individuals, he believed, could not face reality; to endure, one adopts illusions. His attempt to draw lines of continuity from the 13th to the 20th century ended in futility. Adams concluded that all he could prove was change.

In 1908 Adams edited the letters and diary of his friend John Hay, secretary of state from 1898 to 1905. His last book, *The Life of George Cabot Lodge,* was published in 1911. In two speculative essays, "Rule of Phase Applied to History" (1909) and "Letter to American Teachers of History" (1910), Adams calculated the demise of the world. Basing his theory on a scientific law, the dissipation of energy, he described civilization as having retrogressed through four stages: the religious, mechanical, electrical, and ethereal. The cataclysm, he prophesied, would occur in 1921. How literally Adams intended his prediction remains a point of dispute.

In 1912, at the age of 74, Adams suffered a stroke. His haunting fear of senility became real for a short time. For three months he lay partially paralyzed, his mind hovering between reason and delirium. He recovered sufficiently, however, to travel to Europe once again. When he died in 1918, in his sleep in his Washington home, he was, according to his wish, buried next to his wife in an unmarked grave. In 1919 he was posthumously awarded a Pulitzer Prize for the *Education*.

Adams is noted for an ironic literary style coupled with a detached, often bitter, tone. These characteristics have led some critics to view him as an irascible misfit. They contend that his fascination with the Middle Ages and his continuous emphasis upon failure were masks behind which he hid a misanthropic alienation from the world. More sympathetic commentators see Adams as a romantic figure who sought meaning in the chaos and violence of the 20th century. As Adams described it, he was in pursuit of ". . . a world that sensitive and timid natures could regard without a shudder."

Upton Sinclair

The American novelist Upton Sinclair was a polemicist for socialism and other causes; his *The Jungle* is a landmark among naturalistic, proletarian novels.

Born in 1878, Sinclair graduated from the College of the City of New York in 1897 and did graduate work at Columbia University, supporting himself by journalistic writing. *The Jungle* (1906), his sixth novel and first popular success, was written when he was sent by the socialist weekly newspaper *Appeal to Reason* to Chicago to investigate conditions in the stockyards. Though intended to create sympathy for the exploited and poorly treated immigrant workers in the meat-packing industry, *The Jungle* instead aroused widespread public indignation at the quality of and impurities in

Upton Sinclair. Hulton Archive/ Getty Images

processed meats and thus helped bring about the passage of federal food-inspection laws. Sinclair ironically commented at the time, "I aimed at the public's heart and by accident I hit it in the stomach."

The Jungle is the most enduring of the works of the muckrakers. Published at Sinclair's own expense after several publishers rejected it, it became a best-seller, and Sinclair used the proceeds to open Helicon Hall, a cooperative-living venture in Englewood, N.J. The building was destroyed by fire in 1907 and the project abandoned.

A long series of other topical novels followed, none as popular as *The Jungle;* among them were *Oil!* (1927), based on the Teapot Dome Scandal, and *Boston* (1928), based on the Sacco-Vanzetti case. Sinclair's works were highly popular in Russia both before and immediately after the Revolution of 1917. Later his active opposition to the communist regime caused a decline in his reputation there, but it was revived temporarily in the late 1930s and '40s by his antifascist writings. Sinclair again reached a wide audience with the Lanny Budd series, 11 contemporary historical novels beginning with *World's End* (1940) that were constructed around an implausible antifascist hero who happens to be on hand for all the momentous events of the day.

During the economic crisis of the 1930s, Sinclair organized the EPIC (End

A promotional poster for Upton Sinclair's The Jungle. *Library of Congress Prints and Photographs Division*

Muckraker

The name *muckraker* was first applied to a group of American writers identified with pre–World War I reform and exposé literature. The muckrakers provided detailed, accurate journalistic accounts of the political and economic corruption and social hardships caused by the power of big business in a rapidly industrializing United States. The word *muckraker* was pejorative when used by Pres. Theodore Roosevelt in his speech of April 14, 1906; he borrowed a passage from John Bunyan's *Pilgrim's Progress,* which referred to "the Man with the Muckrake . . . who could look no way but downward." But it also came to take on favourable connotations of social concern and courageous exposition.

The muckrakers' work grew out of the yellow journalism of the 1890s, which whetted the public appetite for news arrestingly presented, and out of popular magazines, especially those established by S.S. McClure, Frank A. Munsey, and Peter F. Collier. The emergence of muckraking was heralded in the January 1903 issue of *McClure's Magazine* by articles on municipal government, labour, and trusts, written by Lincoln Steffens, Ray Stannard Baker, and Ida M. Tarbell.

The intense public interest aroused by articles critical of political corruption, industrial monopolies, and fraudulent business practices rallied journalists, novelists, and reformers of all sorts to sharpen their criticism of American society. Charles Edward Russell led the reform writers with exposés ranging from *The Greatest Trust in the World* (1905) to *The Uprising of the Many* (1907), the latter reporting methods being tried to extend democracy in other countries. Lincoln Steffens wrote on corrupt city and state politics in *The Shame of the Cities* (1904). Brand Whitlock, who wrote *The Turn of the Balance* (1907), a novel opposing capital punishment, was also a reform mayor of Toledo, Ohio. Thomas W. Lawson, a Boston financier, in "Frenzied Finance" (*Everybody's,* 1904–05), provided a major exposé of stock-market abuses and insurance fraud. Ida M. Tarbell's *History of the Standard Oil Company* (1904) exposed the corrupt practices used to form a great industrial monopoly. Edwin Markham's *Children in Bondage* was a major attack on child labour. Upton Sinclair's novel *The Jungle* (1906) and Samuel Hopkins Adams's *Great American Fraud* (1906), combined with the work of Harvey W. Wiley and Senator Albert J. Beveridge, brought about passage of the Meat Inspection Act and the Pure Food and Drug Act. David Graham Phillips' series "The Treason of the Senate" (*Cosmopolitan*, 1906), which inspired President Roosevelt's speech in 1906, was influential in leading to the passage of the Seventeenth Amendment to the Constitution, providing for popular senatorial elections. Muckraking as a movement largely disappeared between 1910 and 1912, although the name survived and came to be applied to any writer who exposed corruption and the abuse of power.

Poverty in California) socialist reform movement; in 1934 he was defeated as Democratic candidate for governor. Sinclair withdrew from public life for over a decade before his death in 1968. Of his autobiographical writings, *American Outpost: A Book of Reminiscences* (1932; also published as *Candid Reminiscences: My First Thirty Years*) was reworked and extended in *The Autobiography of Upton Sinclair* (1962); *My Lifetime in Letters* (1960) is a collection of letters written to Sinclair.

POETS OF THE ERA

The later 19th century and early years of the 20th century were a poor period for American poetry; yet (in addition to William Vaughn Moody) two poets of distinction wrote songs that survived long after scores of minor poets had been forgotten. One was Southern-born Sidney Lanier, a talented musician who utilized the rhythms of music and the thematic developments of symphonies in such fine songs as "Corn" (1875), "The Symphony" (1875), and "The Marshes

of Glynn" (1878). Distressed, like many of his contemporaries, by changes in American life, he wove his doubts,
fears, and suggestions into his richest poems.

The other poet was a New Englander, Emily
Dickinson. A shy, playful, odd personality, she allowed
practically none of her writings to be published during her
lifetime. Not until 1890, four years after her death, was
the first book of her poems published, to be followed at
intervals by other collections. Later poets were to be influenced by her individual techniques—use of imperfect, or
eye, rhymes, avoidance of regular rhythms, and a tendency
to pack brief stanzas with cryptic meanings. Like Lanier,
she rediscovered the value of conceits for setting forth
her thoughts and feelings. Such poems as "The Snake," "I
Like to See It Lap the Miles," "The Chariot," "Farther in
Summer than the Birds," and "There's a Certain Slant of
Light" represented her unusual talent at its best.

SIDNEY LANIER

(b. Feb. 3, 1842, Macon, Ga., U.S. — d. Sept. 7, 1881, Lynn, N.C.)

Sidney Lanier was an American musician and poet whose
verse often suggests the rhythms and thematic development of music.

Lanier was reared by devoutly religious parents in the
traditions of the Old South. As a child he wrote verses and
was especially fond of music. After graduation in 1860
from Oglethorpe College (now University), Atlanta, Ga.,
he served in the Civil War until his capture and subsequent
imprisonment at Point Lookout, Md., where he contracted tuberculosis. In 1867 he married Mary Day, also of
Macon; and in the same year he published his first book,
the novel *Tiger-Lilies,* a mixture of German philosophy,
Southern traditional romance, and his own war experiences. After working in his father's law office at Macon,

Sidney Lanier, c. *1870–80.* Courtesy of the Library of Congress, Washington, D.C.

teaching school at Prattville, Ala., and traveling for his health in Texas, he accepted in 1873 a position as first flutist in the Peabody Orchestra, Baltimore. With numerous poems already published in magazines, he wrote several potboilers and played private concerts and delivered lectures to small groups.

"Corn" (1875), a poem treating agricultural conditions in the South, and "The Symphony" (1875), treating industrial conditions in the North, brought Lanier national recognition. Adverse criticism of his "Centennial Meditation" in 1876 launched him on an investigation of verse technique that he continued until his death. *The Song of the Chattahoochee,* a volume of poems, was published in 1877. Appointed to Johns Hopkins University in 1879, he delivered a series of lectures on verse technique, the early English poets, and the English novel, later published as *The Science of English Verse* (1880), *Shakspere and his Forerunners* (1902), and *The English Novel* (1883; rev. ed. 1897). In the spring of 1881, when advanced tuberculosis made further work impossible, he established camp quarters at Lynn, N.C., where he died. Three years later his wife published an enlarged edition of his poems. The complete edition of his works (10 volumes) appeared in 1945.

EMILY DICKINSON
(b. Dec. 10, 1830, Amherst, Mass., U.S.—d. May 15, 1886, Amherst)

The American lyric poet Emily Dickinson lived in seclusion and commanded a singular brilliance of style and integrity of vision. With Walt Whitman, Dickinson is widely considered to be one of the two leading 19th-century American poets.

Only 10 of Emily Dickinson's nearly 1,800 poems are known to have been published in her lifetime. Devoted to private pursuits, she sent hundreds of poems to friends and correspondents while apparently keeping the greater number to herself. She habitually worked in verse forms suggestive of hymns and ballads, with lines of three or four stresses. Her unusual off-rhymes have been seen as both experimental and influenced by the 18th-century hymnist Isaac Watts. She freely ignored the usual rules of versification and even of grammar, and in the intellectual content of her work she likewise proved exceptionally bold and original. Her verse is distinguished by its epigrammatic compression, haunting personal voice, enigmatic brilliance, and lack of high polish.

EARLY YEARS

The second of three children, Dickinson grew up in moderate privilege and with strong local and religious attachments. For her first nine years she resided in a mansion built by her paternal grandfather, Samuel Fowler Dickinson, who had helped found Amherst College but then went bankrupt shortly before her birth. Her father, Edward Dickinson, was a forceful and prosperous Whig lawyer who served as treasurer of the college and was elected to one term in Congress. Her mother, Emily Norcross Dickinson, from the leading family in nearby

Monson, was an introverted wife and hardworking house-keeper; her letters seem equally inexpressive and quirky. Both parents were loving but austere, and Emily became closely attached to her brother, Austin, and sister, Lavinia. Never marrying, the two sisters remained at home, and when their brother married, he and his wife established their own household next door. The highly distinct and even eccentric personalities developed by the three siblings seem to have mandated strict limits to their intimacy. "If we had come up for the first time from two wells," Emily once said of Lavinia, "her astonishment would not be greater at some things I say." Only after the poet's death did Lavinia and Austin realize how dedicated she was to her art.

As a girl, Emily was seen as frail by her parents and others and was often kept home from school. She attended the coeducational Amherst Academy, where she was recognized by teachers and students alike for her prodigious abilities in composition. She also excelled in other subjects emphasized by the school, most notably Latin and the sciences. A class in botany inspired her to assemble an herbarium containing a large number of pressed plants identified by their Latin names. She was fond of her teachers, but when she left home to attend Mount Holyoke Female Seminary (now Mount Holyoke College) in nearby South Hadley, she found the school's institutional tone uncongenial. Mount Holyoke's strict rules and invasive religious practices, along with her own homesickness and growing rebelliousness, help explain why she did not return for a second year.

At home as well as at school and church, the religious faith that ruled the poet's early years was evangelical Calvinism, a faith centred on the belief that humans are born totally depraved and can be saved only if they undergo a life-altering conversion in which they accept the vicarious sacrifice of Jesus Christ. Questioning this tradition soon after leaving Mount Holyoke, Dickinson was to be the only member of her family who did not experience conversion or join Amherst's First Congregational Church. Yet she seems to have retained a belief in the soul's immortality or at least to have transmuted it into a Romantic quest for the transcendent and absolute. One reason her mature religious views elude specification is that she took no interest in creedal or doctrinal definition. In this she was influenced by both the Transcendentalism of Ralph Waldo Emerson and the mid-century tendencies of liberal Protestant orthodoxy. These influences pushed her toward a more symbolic understanding of religious truth and helped shape her vocation as poet.

Development as a Poet

Although Dickinson had begun composing verse by her late teens, few of her early poems are extant. Among them are two of the burlesque "Valentines"—the exuberantly inventive expressions of affection and esteem she sent to friends of her youth. Two other poems dating from the first half of the 1850s draw a contrast between the world as it is and a more peaceful alternative, variously eternity or a serene imaginative order. All her known juvenilia were sent to friends and engage in a striking play of visionary fancies, a direction in which she was encouraged by the popular, sentimental book of essays *Reveries of a Bachelor: Or a Book of the Heart* by Ik. Marvel (the pseudonym of Donald Grant Mitchell). Dickinson's acts of fancy and reverie, however, were more intricately social than those of Marvel's bachelor, uniting the pleasures of solitary mental play, performance for an audience, and intimate communion with another. It may be because her writing began with a strong social impetus that her later solitude did not lead to a meaningless hermeticism.

Until Dickinson was in her mid-20s, her writing mostly took the form of letters, and a surprising number of those that she wrote from age 11 onward have been preserved. Sent to her brother, Austin, or to friends of her own sex, especially Abiah Root, Jane Humphrey, and Susan Gilbert (who would marry Austin), these generous communications overflow with humour, anecdote, invention, and sombre reflection. In general, Dickinson seems to have given and demanded more from her correspondents than she received. On occasion she interpreted her correspondents' laxity in replying as evidence of neglect or even betrayal. Indeed, the loss of friends, whether through death or cooling interest, became a basic pattern for Dickinson. Much of her writing, both poetic and epistolary, seems premised on a feeling of abandonment and a matching effort to deny, overcome, or reflect on a sense of solitude.

Emily Dickinson. Hulton Archive/ Getty Images

Dickinson's closest friendships usually had a literary flavour. She was introduced to the poetry of Ralph Waldo Emerson by one of her father's law students, Benjamin F. Newton, and to that of Elizabeth Barrett Browning by Susan Gilbert and Henry Vaughan Emmons, a gifted college student. Two of Barrett Browning's works, *A Vision of Poets,* describing the pantheon of poets, and *Aurora Leigh*, on the development of a female poet, seem to have played a formative role for Dickinson, validating the idea of female greatness and stimulating her ambition. Though she also corresponded with Josiah G. Holland, a popular writer of the time, he counted for less with her than his appealing wife, Elizabeth, a lifelong friend and the recipient of many affectionate letters.

In 1855 Dickinson traveled to Washington, D.C., with her sister and father, who was then ending his term as U.S. representative. On the return trip the sisters made an extended stay in Philadelphia, where it is thought the poet heard the preaching of Charles Wadsworth, a fascinating Presbyterian minister whose pulpit oratory suggested (as a colleague put it) "years of conflict and agony." Seventy years later, Martha Dickinson Bianchi, the poet's niece, claimed that Emily had fallen in love with Wadsworth, who was married, and then grandly renounced him. The story is too highly coloured for its details to be credited; certainly, there is no evidence the minister returned the poet's love. Yet it is true that a correspondence arose between the two and that Wadsworth visited her in Amherst about 1860 and again in 1880. After his death in 1882, Dickinson remembered him as "my Philadelphia," "my dearest earthly friend," and "my Shepherd from 'Little Girl'hood."

Always fastidious, Dickinson began to restrict her social activity in her early 20s, staying home from communal functions and cultivating intense epistolary relationships with a reduced number of correspondents. In 1855, leaving the large and much-loved house (since razed) in which she had lived for 15 years, the 25-year-old woman and her family moved back to the dwelling associated with her first decade: the Dickinson mansion on Main Street in Amherst. Her home for the rest of her life, this large brick house, still standing, has become a favourite destination for her admirers. She found the return profoundly disturbing, and when her mother became incapacitated by a mysterious illness that lasted from 1855 to 1859, both daughters were compelled to give more of themselves to domestic pursuits. Various events outside the home—a bitter Norcross family lawsuit, the financial collapse of the local railroad that had been promoted by the poet's father, and a powerful religious revival that renewed the pressure to "convert"—made the years 1857 and 1858 deeply troubling for Dickinson and promoted her further withdrawal.

MATURE CAREER

In summer 1858, at the height of this period of obscure tension, Dickinson began assembling her manuscript-books. She made clean copies of her poems on fine quality stationery and then sewed small bundles of these sheets together at the fold. Over the next seven years she created 40 such booklets and several unsewn sheaves, and altogether they contained about 800 poems. No doubt she intended to arrange her work in a convenient form, perhaps for her own use in sending poems to friends. Perhaps the assemblage was meant to remain private, like her earlier herbarium. Or perhaps, as implied in a poem of 1863, "This is my letter to the world," she anticipated posthumous publication. Because she left no instructions regarding the disposition of her manuscript-books, her ultimate purpose in assembling them can only be conjectured.

Dickinson sent more poems to her sister-in-law, Susan Gilbert Dickinson, a cultivated reader, than to any other known correspondent. Repeatedly professing eternal allegiance, these poems often imply that there was a certain distance between the two—that the sister-in-law was felt to be haughty, remote, or even incomprehensible. Yet Susan admired the poetry's wit and verve and offered the kind of personally attentive audience Dickinson craved.

On one occasion, Susan's dissatisfaction with a poem, "Safe in their alabaster chambers," resulted in the drafting of alternative stanzas. Susan was an active hostess, and her home was the venue at which Dickinson met a few friends, most importantly Samuel Bowles, publisher and editor of the influential *Springfield Republican*. Gregarious, captivating, and unusually liberal on the question of women's careers, Bowles had a high regard for Dickinson's poems, publishing (without her consent) seven of them during her lifetime—more than appeared in any other outlet. From 1859 to 1862 she sent him some of her most intense and confidential communications, including the daring poem "Title divine is mine," whose speaker proclaims that she is now a "Wife," but of a highly unconventional type.

In those years Dickinson experienced a painful and obscure personal crisis, partly of a romantic nature. The abject and pleading drafts of her second and third letters to the unidentified person she called "Master" are probably related to her many poems about a loved but distant person, usually male. There has been much speculation about the identity of this individual. One of the first candidates was George Henry Gould, the recipient in 1850 of a prose Valentine from Dickinson. Some have contended that Master was a woman, possibly Kate Scott Anthon or Susan Dickinson. Richard Sewall's 1974 biography makes the case for Samuel Bowles. All such claims have rested on a partial examination of surviving documents and collateral evidence. Since it is now believed that the earliest draft to Master predates her friendship with Bowles, he cannot have been the person. On balance, Charles Wadsworth and possibly Gould remain the most likely candidates.

Whoever the person was, Master's failure to return Dickinson's affection—together with Susan's absorption in her first childbirth and Bowles's growing invalidism—contributed to a piercing and ultimate sense of distress. In a letter, Dickinson described her lonely suffering as a "terror—since September—[that] I could tell to none." Instead of succumbing to anguish, however, she came to view it as the sign of a special vocation, and it became the basis of an unprecedented creativity. A poem that seems to register this life-restoring act of resistance begins "The zeroes taught us phosphorus," meaning that it is in absolute cold and nothingness that true brilliance originates.

Though Dickinson wrote little about the American Civil War, which was then raging, her awareness of its multiplied tragedies seems to have empowered her poetic drive. As she confided to her cousins in Boston, apropos of wartime bereavements, "Every day life feels mightier, and what we have the power to be, more stupendous." In the hundreds of poems Dickinson composed during the war, a movement can be discerned from the expression of immediate pain or exultation to the celebration of achievement and self-command. Building on her earlier quest for human intimacy and obsession with heaven, she explored the tragic ironies of human desire, such as fulfillment denied, the frustrated search for the absolute within the mundane, and the terrors of internal dissolution. She also articulated a profound sense of female subjectivity, expressing what it means to be subordinate, secondary, or not in control. Yet as the war proceeded, she also wrote with growing frequency about self-reliance, imperviousness, personal triumph, and hard-won liberty. The perfect transcendence she had formerly associated with heaven was now attached to a vision of supreme artistry.

In April 1862, about the time Wadsworth left the East Coast for a pastorate in San Francisco, Dickinson sought the critical advice of Thomas Wentworth Higginson, whose witty article of advice to writers, "A Letter to a Young

Contributor," had just appeared in *The Atlantic Monthly*. Higginson was known as a writer of delicate nature essays and a crusader for women's rights. Enclosing four poems, Dickinson asked for his opinion of her verse—whether or not it was "alive." The ensuing correspondence lasted for years, with the poet sending her "preceptor," as she called him, many more samples of her work. In addition to seeking an informed critique from a professional but not unsympathetic man of letters, she was reaching out at a time of accentuated loneliness. "You were not aware that you saved my Life," she confided years later.

Dickinson's last trips from Amherst were in 1864 and 1865, when she shared her cousins Louisa and Frances Norcross's boardinghouse in Cambridge and underwent a course of treatment with the leading Boston ophthalmologist. She described her symptoms as an aching in her eyes and a painful sensitivity to light. Of the two posthumous diagnoses, exotropia (a kind of strabismus, the inability of one eye to align with the other) and anterior uveitis (inflammation of the uvea, a part of the iris), the latter seems more likely. In 1869 Higginson invited the poet to Boston to attend a literary salon. The terms she used in declining his invitation—"I do not cross my Father's ground to any House or town"—make clear her refusal by that time to leave home and also reveal her sense of paternal order. When Higginson visited her the next year, he recorded his vivid first impression of her "plain" features, "exquisitely" neat attire, "childlike" manner, and loquacious and exhausting brilliance. He was "glad not to live near her."

In her last 15 years Dickinson averaged 35 poems a year and conducted her social life mainly through her chiselled and often sibylline written messages. Her father's sudden death in 1874 caused a profound and persisting emotional upheaval yet eventually led to a greater openness, self-possession, and serenity. She repaired an 11-year breach with Samuel Bowles and made friends with Maria Whitney, a teacher of modern languages at Smith College, and Helen Hunt Jackson, poet and author of the novel *Ramona* (1884). Dickinson resumed contact with Wadsworth, and from about age 50 she conducted a passionate romance with Otis Phillips Lord, an elderly judge on the supreme court of Massachusetts. The letters she apparently sent Lord reveal her at her most playful, alternately teasing and confiding. In declining an erotic advance or his proposal of marriage, she asked, "Dont you know you are happiest while I withhold and not confer—dont you know that 'No' is the wildest word we consign to Language?"

After Dickinson's aging mother was incapacitated by a stroke and a broken hip, caring for her at home made large demands on the poet's time and patience. After her mother died in 1882, Dickinson summed up the relationship in a confidential letter to her Norcross cousins: "We were never intimate Mother and Children while she was our Mother—but...when she became our Child, the Affection came." The deaths of Dickinson's friends in her last years—Bowles in 1878, Wadsworth in 1882, Lord in 1884, and Jackson in 1885—left her feeling terminally alone. But the single most shattering death, occurring in 1883, was that of her eight-year-old nephew next door, the gifted and charming Gilbert Dickinson. Her health broken by this culminating tragedy, she ceased seeing almost everyone, apparently including her sister-in-law. The poet died in 1886, when she was 55 years old. The immediate cause of death was a stroke. The attending physician attributed this to Bright's disease, but a modern posthumous diagnosis points to severe primary hypertension as the underlying condition.

ASSESSMENT

Dickinson's exact wishes regarding the publication of her poetry are in dispute. When Lavinia found the manuscript-books, she decided the poems should be made public and asked Susan to prepare an edition. Susan failed to move the project forward, however, and after two years Lavinia turned the manuscript-books over to Mabel Loomis Todd, a local family friend, who energetically transcribed and selected the poems and also enlisted the aid of Thomas Wentworth Higginson in editing. A complicating circumstance was that Todd was conducting an affair with Susan's husband, Austin. When *Poems by Emily Dickinson* appeared in 1890, it drew widespread interest and a warm welcome from the eminent American novelist and critic William Dean Howells, who saw the verse as a signal expression of a distinctively American sensibility. But Susan, who was well aware of her husband's ongoing affair with Todd, was outraged at what she perceived as Lavinia's betrayal and Todd's effrontery. The enmity between Susan and Todd, and later between their daughters, Martha Dickinson Bianchi and Millicent Todd Bingham (each of whom edited selections of Dickinson's work), had a pernicious effect on the presentation of Emily Dickinson's work. Her poetic manuscripts are divided between two primary collections: the poems in Bingham's possession went to Amherst College Library, and those in Bianchi's hands to Harvard University's Houghton Library. The acrimonious relationship between the two families has affected scholarly interpretation of Dickinson's work into the 21st century.

In editing Dickinson's poems in the 1890s, Todd and Higginson invented titles and regularized diction, grammar, metre, and rhyme. The first scholarly editions of

Dickinson's poems and letters, by Thomas H. Johnson, did not appear until the 1950s. A much improved edition of the complete poems was brought out in 1998 by R.W. Franklin. A reliable edition of the letters is not yet available.

In spite of her "modernism," Dickinson's verse drew little interest from the first generation of "High Modernists." Hart Crane and Allen Tate were among the first leading writers to register her greatness, followed in the 1950s by Elizabeth Bishop and others. The New Critics also played an important role in establishing her place in the modern canon. From the beginning, however, Dickinson has strongly appealed to many ordinary or unschooled readers. Her unmistakable voice, private yet forthright—"I'm Nobody! Who are you? / Are you— Nobody—too?"—establishes an immediate connection. Readers respond, too, to the impression her poems convey of a haunting private life, one marked by extremes of deprivation and refined ecstasies. At the same time, her rich abundance—her great range of feeling, her supple expressiveness—testifies to an intrinsic poetic genius. Widely translated into Japanese, Italian, French, German, and many other languages, Dickinson has begun to strike readers as the one American lyric poet who belongs in the pantheon with Sappho, Catullus, Saʿdī, the Shakespeare of the sonnets, Rainer Maria Rilke, and Arthur Rimbaud.

CHAPTER 2

AMERICAN NATURALISM

O ther American writers toward the close of the 19th century moved toward naturalism, a more advanced stage of realism. Hamlin Garland's writings exemplified some aspects of this development when he made short stories and novels vehicles for philosophical and social preachments and was franker than Howells in stressing the harsher details of the farmer's struggles and in treating the subject of sex. *Main-Travelled Roads* (1891) and *Rose of Dutcher's Coolly* (1895) displayed Garland's particular talents. These and a critical manifesto for the new fiction, *Crumbling Idols* (1894), were influential contributions to a developing movement.

Other American authors of the same period or slightly later were avowed followers of French naturalists led by Émile Zola. Theodore Dreiser, for instance, treated subjects that had seemed too daring to earlier realists and, like other Naturalists, illustrated his own beliefs by his depictions of characters and unfolding of plots. Holding that men's deeds were "chemical compulsions," he showed characters unable to direct their actions. Holding also that "the race was to the swift and the battle to the strong," he showed characters defeated by stronger and more ruthless opponents. His major books included *Sister Carrie* (1900), *Jennie Gerhardt* (1911), *The Financier* (1912), *The Titan* (1914), and—much later—*An American Tragedy* (1925).

Dreiser did not bother with—or did not care for—niceties of style or elaborate symbolism such as were found in French naturalistic works; but Stephen Crane and Frank Norris were attentive to such matters. In short novels, *Maggie: A Girl of the Streets* (1893) and *The Red Badge of Courage* (1895), and in some of his short stories, Crane was an impressionist who made his details and his setting forth of them embody a conception of man overwhelmed by circumstance and environment. Frank Norris, who admired Crane's "aptitude for making phrases—sparks that cast a momentary gleam upon whole phases of life," himself tried to make phrases, scenes, and whole narratives cast such gleams in *McTeague* (1899), *The Octopus* (1901), and *The Pit* (1903). Both Crane and Norris died young, their full abilities undeveloped but their experiments foreshadowing later achievements in the 20th-century novel.

WILLIAM DEAN HOWELLS

(b. March 1, 1837, Martins Ferry, Ohio, U.S.—d. May 11, 1920, New York, N.Y.)

An American novelist and critic, William Dean Howells was one of the most important figures of late 19th-century American letters, the champion of literary realism, and the close friend and adviser of Mark Twain and Henry James.

The son of an itinerant printer and newspaper editor, Howells grew up in various Ohio towns and began work early as a typesetter and later as a reporter. Meanwhile, he taught himself languages, becoming well read in German, Spanish, and English classics, and began contributing poems to *The Atlantic Monthly*. His campaign biography of Abraham Lincoln (1860) financed a trip to New England, where he met the great men of the literary establishment, James Russell Lowell, editor of *The Atlantic Monthly*, Oliver

Naturalism

In literature and the visual arts, naturalism was a late 19th- and early 20th-century movement that was inspired by adaptation of the principles and methods of natural science, especially the Darwinian view of nature, to literature and art. In literature it extended the tradition of realism, aiming at an even more faithful, unselective representation of reality, a veritable "slice of life," presented without moral judgment. Naturalism differed from realism in its assumption of scientific determinism, which led naturalistic authors to emphasize man's accidental, physiological nature rather than his moral or rational qualities. Individual characters were seen as helpless products of heredity and environment, motivated by strong instinctual drives from within and harassed by social and economic pressures from without. As such, they had little will or responsibility for their fates, and the prognosis for their "cases" was pessimistic at the outset.

Naturalism originated in France and had its direct theoretical basis in the critical approach of Hippolyte Taine, who announced in his introduction to *Histoire de la littérature anglaise* (1863–64; *History of English Literature*) that "there is a cause for ambition, for courage, for truth, as there is for digestion, for muscular movement, for animal heat. Vice and virtue are products, like vitriol and sugar." Though the first "scientific" novel was the Goncourt brothers' case history of a servant girl, *Germinie Lacerteux* (1864), the leading exponent of naturalism was Émile Zola, whose essay "Le Roman expérimental" (1880; "The Experimental Novel") became the literary manifesto of the school. According to Zola, the novelist was no longer to be a mere observer, content to record phenomena, but a detached experimenter who subjects his characters and their passions to a series of tests and who works with emotional and social facts as a chemist works with matter. Upon Zola's example the naturalistic style became widespread and affected to varying degrees most of the major writers of the period. Guy de Maupassant's popular story "The Necklace" heralds the introduction of a character who is to be treated like a specimen under a micro-scope. The early works of Joris-Karl Huysmans, of the German dramatist Gerhart Hauptmann, and of the Portuguese novelist José Maria Eça de Queirós were based on the precepts of naturalism.

The Théâtre Libre was founded in Paris in 1887 by André Antoine and the Freie Bühne of Berlin in 1889 by Otto Brahm to present plays dealing with the new themes of naturalism in a naturalistic style with naturalistic staging. A parallel develop-ment occurred in the visual arts. Painters, following the lead of the realist painter Gustave Courbet, were choosing themes from contemporary life. Many of them deserted the studio for the open air, finding subjects among the peasants and tradesmen in the street and capturing them as they found them, unpremedi-tated and unposed. One result of this approach was that their finished canvases had the freshness and immediacy of sketches. Zola, the spokesman for literary naturalism, was also the first to champion Édouard Manet and the Impressionists.

Despite their claim to complete objectivity, the literary nat-uralists were handicapped by certain biases inherent in their deterministic theories. Though they faithfully reflected nature, it was always a nature "red in tooth and claw." Their views on heredity gave them a predilection for simple characters domi-nated by strong, elemental passions. Their views on the overpowering effects of environment led them to select for sub-jects the most oppressive environments—the slums or the underworld—and they documented these milieus, often in dreary and sordid detail. The drab palette of Vincent van Gogh's naturalistic painting *The Potato Eaters* (1885; Rijksmuseum, Amsterdam) was the palette of literary naturalism. Finally, they were unable to suppress an element of romantic protest against the social conditions they described.

As a historical movement, naturalism per se was short-lived; but it contributed to art an enrichment of realism, new areas of subject matter, and a largeness and formlessness that was indeed closer to life than to art. Its multiplicity of impressions conveyed the sense of a world in constant flux, inevitably junglelike, because it teemed with interdependent lives.

In American literature, naturalism had a delayed blooming in the work of Hamlin Garland, Stephen Crane, Frank Norris, and Jack London; and it reached its peak in the art of Theodore Dreiser. James T. Farrell's Studs Lonigan trilogy (1932–35) is one of the latest expressions of true naturalism.

Wendell Holmes, Hawthorne, and Emerson. On Lincoln's victory he was rewarded with a consulship at Venice (1861–65), which enabled him to marry. On his return to the U.S. he became assistant editor (1866–71), then editor (1871–81), of *The Atlantic Monthly*, in which he began publishing reviews and articles that interpreted American writers. He was a shrewd judge of his contemporaries. He immediately recognized the worth of Henry James, and he was the first to take Mark Twain seriously as an artist.

Their Wedding Journey (1872) and *A Chance Acquaintance* (1873) were his first realistic novels of uneventful middle-class life. There followed some international novels, contrasting American and European manners. Howells's best work depicts the American scene as it changed from a simple, egalitarian society where luck and pluck were rewarded to one in which social and economic gulfs were becoming unbridgeable, and the individual's fate was ruled by chance.

William Dean Howells, 1913.
Courtesy of the Library of Congress, Washington, D.C.

He wrote *A Modern Instance* (1882), the story of the disintegration of a marriage, which is considered his strongest novel. His best known work, *The Rise of Silas Lapham* (1885), deals with a self-made businessman's efforts to fit into Boston society. In 1887 he risked both livelihood and reputation with his plea for clemency for the condemned Haymarket anarchists on the grounds that they had been convicted for their political beliefs. In 1888 he left Boston for New York.

His deeply shaken social faith is reflected in the novels of his New York period, such as the strongly pro-labour *Annie Kilburn* (1888) and *A Hazard of New Fortunes* (1890), generally considered his finest work, which dramatizes the teeming, competitive life of New York, where a representative group of characters try to establish a magazine.

Howells's critical writings of this period welcomed the young naturalistic novelists Hamlin Garland, Stephen Crane, and Frank Norris and promoted the European authors Turgenev, Ibsen, Zola, Pérez Galdós, Verga, and above all Tolstoy.

Long before his death Howells was out of fashion. Later critics have more fairly evaluated his enormous influence, and readers have rediscovered the style, humour, and honesty of his best works.

THEODORE DREISER

(b. Aug. 27, 1871, Terre Haute, Ind., U.S.—d. Dec. 28, 1945, Hollywood, Calif.)

The novelist Theodore Dreiser was the outstanding American practitioner of naturalism. He was the leading figure in a national literary movement that replaced the observance of Victorian notions of propriety with the unflinching presentation of real-life subject matter. Among other themes, his novels explore the new social problems that had arisen in a rapidly industrializing America.

LIFE

Dreiser was the ninth of 10 surviving children in a family whose perennial poverty forced frequent moves between small Indiana towns and Chicago in search of a lower cost of living. His father, a German immigrant, was a mostly unemployed millworker who subscribed to a stern and narrow Roman Catholicism. His mother's gentle and compassionate outlook sprang from her Czech Mennonite background. In later life Dreiser would bitterly associate religion with his father's ineffectuality and the family's resulting material deprivation, but he always spoke and wrote of his mother with unswerving affection. Dreiser's own harsh experience of poverty as a youth and his early yearnings for wealth and success would become dominant themes in his novels, and the misadventures of his brothers and sisters in early adult life gave him additional material on which to base his characters.

Dreiser's spotty education in parochial and public schools was capped by a year (1889–90) at Indiana University. He began a career as a newspaper reporter in Chicago in 1892 and worked his way to the

Theodore Dreiser. Apic/Hulton Archive/Getty Images

East Coast. While writing for a Pittsburgh newspaper in 1894, he read works by the scientists T. H. Huxley and John Tyndall and adopted the speculations of the philosopher Herbert Spencer. Through these readings and his own experience, Dreiser came to believe that human beings are helpless in the grip of instincts and social forces beyond their control, and he judged human society as an unequal contest between the strong and the weak. In 1894 Dreiser arrived in New York City, where he worked for several newspapers and contributed to magazines. He married Sara White in 1898, but his roving affections (and resulting infidelities) doomed their relationship. The couple separated permanently in 1912.

Dreiser began writing his first novel, *Sister Carrie*, in 1899 at the suggestion of a newspaper colleague. Doubleday, Page, and Company published it the following year, thanks in large measure to the enthusiasm of that firm's reader, the novelist Frank Norris. But Doubleday's qualms about the book, the story line of which involves a young kept woman whose "immorality" goes unpunished, led the publisher to limit the book's advertising, and consequently it sold fewer than 500 copies. This disappointment and an accumulation of family and marital troubles sent Dreiser into a suicidal depression from which he was rescued in 1901 by his brother, Paul Dresser, a well-known songwriter, who arranged for Theodore's treatment in a sanitarium. Dreiser recovered his spirits, and in the next nine years he achieved notable financial success as an editor in chief of several women's magazines. He was forced to resign in 1910, however, because of an office imbroglio involving his romantic fascination with an assistant's daughter.

Somewhat encouraged by the earlier response to *Sister Carrie* in England and the novel's republication in America,

Dreiser returned to writing fiction. The reception accorded his second novel, *Jennie Gerhardt* (1911), the story of a woman who submits sexually to rich and powerful men to help her poverty-stricken family, lent him further encouragement. The first two volumes of a projected trilogy of novels based on the life of the American transportation magnate Charles T. Yerkes, *The Financier* (1912) and *The Titan* (1914), followed. Dreiser recorded his experiences on a trip to Europe in *A Traveler at Forty* (1913). In his next major novel, *The 'Genius'* (1915), he transformed his own life and numerous love affairs into a sprawling semiautobiographical chronicle that was censured by the New York Society for the Suppression of Vice. There ensued 10 years of sustained literary activity during which Dreiser produced a short-story collection, *Free and Other Stories* (1918); a book of sketches, *Twelve Men* (1919); philosophical essays, *Hey-Rub-a-Dub-Dub* (1920); a rhapsodic description of New York, *The Color of A Great City* (1923); works of drama, including *Plays of the Natural and Supernatural* (1916) and *The Hand of the Potter* (1918); and the autobiographical works *A Hoosier Holiday* (1916) and *A Book About Myself* (1922).

In 1925 Dreiser's first novel in a decade, *An American Tragedy*, based on a celebrated murder case, was published. This book brought Dreiser a degree of critical and commercial success he had never before attained and would not thereafter equal. The book's highly critical view of the American legal system also made him the adopted champion of social reformers. He became involved in a variety of causes and slackened his literary production. A visit to the Soviet Union in 1927 produced a skeptical critique of that communist society entitled *Dreiser Looks at Russia* (1928). His only other significant publications in the late 1920s were collections of stories and sketches written earlier, *Chains* (1927) and *A Gallery of Women* (1929), and an unsuccessful collection of poetry, *Moods, Cadenced and Declaimed* (1926).

The Great Depression of the 1930s ended Dreiser's prosperity and intensified his commitment to social causes. He came to reconsider his opposition to communism and wrote the anticapitalist *Tragic America* (1931). His only important literary achievement in this decade was the autobiography of his childhood and teens, *Dawn* (1931), one of the most candid self-revelations by any major writer. In the middle and late '30s his growing social consciousness and his interest in science converged to produce a vaguely mystical philosophy.

In 1938 Dreiser moved from New York to Los Angeles with Helen Richardson, who had been his mistress since 1920. There he set about marketing the film rights to his earlier works. In 1942 he began belatedly to rewrite *The Bulwark*, a novel begun in 1912. The task was completed in 1944, the same year he married Helen. (Sara White Dreiser had died in 1942.) One of his last acts was to join the American Communist Party. Helen helped him complete most of *The Stoic*, the long-postponed third volume of his Yerkes trilogy, in the weeks before his death. Both *The Bulwark* and *The Stoic* were published posthumously (1946 and 1947, respectively). A collection of Dreiser's philosophical speculations, *Notes on Life*, appeared in 1974.

WORKS

Dreiser's first novel, *Sister Carrie* (1900), is a work of pivotal importance in American literature despite its inauspicious launching. It became a beacon to subsequent American writers whose allegiance was to the realistic treatment of any and all subject matter. *Sister Carrie* tells the story of a rudderless but pretty small-town girl who comes to the big city filled with vague ambitions. She is used by men and uses them in turn to become a successful Broadway actress while George Hurstwood, the married man who has run away with her, loses his grip on life and descends into beggary and suicide. *Sister Carrie* was the first masterpiece of the American naturalistic movement in its grittily factual presentation of the vagaries of urban life and in its ingenuous heroine, who goes unpunished for her transgressions against conventional sexual morality. The book's strengths include a brooding but compassionate view of humanity, a memorable cast of characters, and a compelling narrative line. The emotional disintegration of Hurstwood is a much-praised triumph of psychological analysis.

Dreiser's second novel, *Jennie Gerhardt* (1911), is a lesser achievement than *Sister Carrie* owing to its heroine's comparative lack of credibility. Based on Dreiser's remembrance of his beloved mother, Jennie emerges as a plaster saint with whom most modern readers find it difficult to empathize. The novel's strengths include stinging characterizations of social snobs and narrow "religionists," as well as a deep sympathy for the poor.

The Financier (1912) and *The Titan* (1914) are the first two novels of a trilogy dealing with the career of the late-19th century American financier and traction tycoon Charles T. Yerkes, who is cast in fictionalized form as Frank Cowperwood. As Cowperwood successfully plots monopolistic business coups first in Philadelphia and then in Chicago, the focus of the novels alternates between his amoral business dealings and his marital and other erotic relations. *The Financier* and *The Titan* are important examples of the business novel and represent probably the most meticulously researched and documented studies of high finance in first-rate fiction. Cowperwood, like all of Dreiser's major characters, remains unfulfilled despite achieving most of his apparent wishes. The third novel in the trilogy, *The Stoic* (1947), is fatally weakened by Dreiser's diminished interest in his protagonist.

The 'Genius' (1915) is artistically one of Dreiser's least successful novels but is nonetheless indispensable to an understanding of his psychology. This book chronicles its autobiographical hero's career as an artist and his unpredictable pursuit of the perfect woman as a source of ultimate fulfillment.

Dreiser's longest novel, *An American Tragedy* (1925), is a complex and compassionate account of the life and death of a young antihero named Clyde Griffiths. The novel begins with Clyde's blighted background, recounts his path to success, and culminates in his apprehension, trial, and execution for murder. The book was called by one influential critic "the worst-written great novel in the world," but its questionable grammar and style are transcended by its narrative power. Dreiser's labyrinthine speculations on the extent of Clyde's guilt do not blunt his searing indictment of materialism and the American dream of success.

Dreiser's next-to-last novel, *The Bulwark* (1946), is the story of a Quaker father's unavailing struggle to shield his children from the materialism of modern American life. More intellectually consistent than Dreiser's earlier novels, this book also boasts some of his most polished prose.

ASSESSMENT

Dreiser's considerable stature, beyond his historic importance as a pioneer of unvarnished truth-telling in modern literature, is due almost entirely to his achievements as a novelist. His sprawling imagination and cumbersome style kept him from performing well in the smaller literary forms, and his nonfiction writing, especially his essays, are marred by intellectual inconsistency, a lack of objectivity, and even bitterness. But these latter traits are much less obtrusive in his novels, where his compassion and empathy for human striving make his best work moving and memorable. The long novel gave Dreiser the prime form through which to explore in depth the possibilities of 20th-century American life, with its material profusion and spiritual doubt. Dreiser's characters struggle for self-realization in the face of society's narrow and repressive moral conventions, and they often obtain material success and erotic gratification while a more enduring spiritual satisfaction eludes them. Despite Dreiser's alleged deficiencies as a stylist, his novels succeed in their accumulation of realistic detail and in the power and integrity with which they delineate the tragic aspects of the American pursuit of worldly success. *Sister Carrie* and *An American Tragedy* are certainly enduring works of literature that display a deep understanding of the American experience around the turn of the century, with its expansive desires and pervasive disillusionments.

STEPHEN CRANE

(b. Nov. 1, 1871, Newark, N.J., U.S. — d. June 5, 1900, Badenweiler, Baden, Ger.)

An American novelist, poet, and short-story writer, Stephen Crane is best known for his novels *Maggie: A Girl of the Streets* (1893) and *The Red Badge of Courage* (1895) and the short stories "The Open Boat," "The Bride Comes to Yellow Sky," and "The Blue Hotel."

Stephen's father, Jonathan Crane, was a Methodist minister who died in 1880, leaving Stephen, the youngest of 14 children, to be reared by his devout, strong-minded mother. After attending preparatory school at the Claverack College (1888–90), Crane spent less than two

Stephen Crane, 1897. Stephen Crane Collection, Syracuse University Library Department of Special Collections

years at college and then went to New York City to live in a medical students' boardinghouse while freelancing his way to a literary career. While alternating bohemian student life and explorations of the Bowery slums with visits to genteel relatives in the country near Port Jervis, N.Y., Crane wrote his first book, *Maggie: A Girl of the Streets* (1893), a sympathetic study of an innocent and abused slum girl's descent into prostitution and her eventual suicide.

At that time so shocking that Crane published it under a pseudonym and at his own expense, *Maggie* left him to struggle as a poor and unknown freelance journalist, until he was befriended by Hamlin Garland and the influential critic William Dean Howells. Suddenly in 1895 the publication of *The Red Badge of Courage* and of his first book of poems, *The Black Riders,* brought him international fame. Strikingly different in tone and technique from *Maggie, The Red Badge of Courage* is a subtle impressionistic study of a young soldier trying to find reality amid the conflict of fierce warfare. The book's hero, Henry Fleming, survives his own fear, cowardice, and vainglory and goes on to discover courage, humility, and perhaps wisdom in the confused combat of an unnamed Civil War battle. Crane, who had as yet seen no war, was widely praised by veterans for his uncanny power to imagine and reproduce the sense of actual combat.

Crane's few remaining years were chaotic and personally disastrous. His unconventionality and his sympathy for the downtrodden aroused malicious gossip and false charges of drug addiction and Satanism that disgusted the fastidious author. His reputation as a war writer, his desire to see if he had guessed right about the psychology of combat, and his fascination with death and danger sent him to Greece and then to Cuba as a war correspondent.

His first attempt in 1897 to report on the insurrection in Cuba ended in near disaster; the ship *Commodore* on which he was traveling sank with $5,000 worth of ammunition, and Crane—reported drowned—finally rowed into shore in a dinghy with the captain, cook, and oiler, Crane scuttling his money belt of gold before swimming through dangerous surf. The result was one of the world's great short stories, "The Open Boat."

Unable to get to Cuba, Crane went to Greece to report the Greco-Turkish War for the New York *Journal*. He was accompanied by Cora Taylor, a former brothel-house proprietor. At the end of the war they settled in England in a villa at Oxted, Surrey, and in April 1898 Crane departed to report the Spanish-American War in Cuba, first for the New York *World* and then for the New York *Journal*. When the war ended, Crane wrote the first draft of *Active Service*, a novel of the Greek war. He finally returned to Cora in England nine months after his departure and settled in a costly 14th-century manor house at Brede Place, Sussex. Here Cora, a silly woman with social and literary pretensions, contributed to Crane's ruin by encouraging his own social ambitions. They ruined themselves financially by entertaining hordes of spongers, as well as close literary friends—including Joseph Conrad, Ford Madox Ford, H.G. Wells, Henry James, and Robert Barr, who completed Crane's Irish romance *The O'Ruddy*.

Crane now fought a desperate battle against time, illness, and debts. Privation and exposure in his Bowery years and as a correspondent, together with an almost deliberate disregard for his health, probably hastened the disease that killed him at an early age. He died of tuberculosis that was compounded by the recurrent malarial fever he had caught in Cuba.

After *The Red Badge of Courage*, Crane's few attempts at the novel were of small importance, but he achieved an extraordinary mastery of the short story. He exploited youthful small-town experiences in *The Monster and Other*

Stories (1899) and *Whilomville Stories* (1900); the Bowery again in *George's Mother* (1896); an early trip to the southwest and Mexico in "The Blue Hotel" and "The Bride Comes to Yellow Sky"; the Civil War again in *The Little Regiment* (1896); and war correspondent experiences in *The Open Boat and Other Tales of Adventure* (1898) and *Wounds in the Rain* (1900). In the best of these tales Crane showed a rare ability to shape colourful settings, dramatic action, and perceptive characterization into ironic explorations of human nature and destiny. In even briefer scope, rhymeless, cadenced and "free" in form, his unique, flashing poetry was extended into *War Is Kind* (1899).

Stephen Crane first broke new ground in *Maggie,* which evinced an uncompromising (then considered sordid) realism that initiated the literary trend of the succeeding generations—i.e., the sociological novels of Frank Norris, Theodore Dreiser, and James T. Farrell. Crane intended *The Red Badge of Courage* to be "a psychological portrayal of fear," and reviewers rightly praised its psychological realism. The first nonromantic novel of the Civil War to attain widespread popularity, *The Red Badge of Courage* turned the tide of the prevailing convention about war fiction and established a new, if not unprecedented, one. The secret of Crane's success as war correspondent, journalist, novelist, short-story writer, and poet lay in his achieving tensions between irony and pity, illusion and reality, or the double mood of hope contradicted by despair. Crane was a great stylist and a master of the contradictory effect.

FRANK NORRIS

(b. March 5, 1870, Chicago, Ill., U.S.—d. Oct. 25, 1902, San Francisco, Calif.)

Frank Norris was an American novelist who was the first important naturalist writer in the United States.

Norris studied painting in Paris for two years but then decided that literature was his vocation. He attended the University of California in 1890–94 and then spent another year at Harvard University. He was a news correspondent in South Africa in 1895, an editorial assistant on the *San Francisco Wave* (1896–97), and a war correspondent in Cuba for *McClure's Magazine* in 1898. He joined the New York City publishing firm of Doubleday, Page, and Company in 1899. He died three years later after an operation for appendicitis.

Norris's first important novel, *McTeague* (1899), is a naturalist work set in San Francisco. It tells the story of a brutal dentist who murders his miserly wife and then meets his own end while fleeing through Death Valley. With this book and those that followed, Norris joined Theodore Dreiser in the front rank of American novelists. Norris's masterpiece, *The Octopus* (1901), was the first novel of a projected trilogy, *The Epic of the Wheat*, dealing with the economic and social forces involved in the production, distribution, and consumption of wheat. *The Octopus* pictures with bold symbolism the raising of wheat in California and the struggle of the wheat growers there against a monopolistic railway corporation. The second novel in the trilogy, *The Pit* (1903), deals with wheat speculation on the Chicago Board of Trade. The third novel, *Wolf*, unwritten at Norris's death, was to have shown the American-grown wheat relieving a famine-stricken village in Europe. *Vandover and the Brute*, posthumously published in 1914, is a study of degeneration. *McTeague* was filmed by Erich von Stroheim in 1924 under the title *Greed* and staged as an opera by composer William Bolcom and director Robert Altman in 1992.

After the example of Émile Zola and the European naturalists, Norris in *McTeague* sought to describe with realistic detail the influence of heredity and environment on human life. From *The Octopus* on he adopted a more humanitarian ideal and began to view the novel as a proper agent for social betterment. In *The Octopus* and other novels he strove to return American fiction, which was then dominated by historical romance, to more serious themes. Despite their romanticizing tendencies, his novels present a vividly authentic and highly readable picture of life in California at the turn of the 20th century.

Norris's writings were collected (10 vol.) in 1928, and *The Letters of Frank Norris* was edited by Franklin Walker in 1956.

HENRY JAMES

(b. April 15, 1843, New York, N.Y., U.S.—d. Feb. 28, 1916, London, Eng.)

In the books of Henry James, fiction took a different pathway from that of the other naturalists. Like realists and naturalists of his time, he thought that fiction should reproduce reality. He conceived of reality, however, as twice translated—first, through the author's peculiar experiencing of it and, second, through his unique depicting of it. Deep insight and thorough experience were no more important, therefore, than the complicated and delicate task of the artist. *The Art of Fiction* (1884), essays on novelists, and brilliant prefaces to his collected works showed him struggling thoroughly and consciously with the problems of his craft. Together, they formed an important body of discussion of fictional artistry.

An excellent short-story writer, James nevertheless was chiefly important for novels in which his doctrines found concrete embodiment. Outstanding were *The American* (1877), *The Portrait of a Lady* (1881), *The Spoils of Poynton* (1897), *What Maisie Knew* (1897), *The Wings of the Dove* (1902), *The Ambassadors* (1903), and *The Golden Bowl*

(1904). The earliest of these were international novels wherein conflicts arose from relationships between Americans and Europeans—each group with its own characteristics and morals. As time passed, he became increasingly interested in the psychological processes of his characters and in a subtle rendering of their limited insights, their perceptions, and their emotions.

EARLY LIFE AND WORKS

Henry James was named for his father, a prominent social theorist and lecturer, and was the younger brother of the pragmatist philosopher William James. The young Henry was a shy, book-addicted boy who assumed the role of quiet observer beside his active elder brother. They were taken abroad as infants, were schooled by tutors and governesses, and spent their preadolescent years in Manhattan. Returned to Geneva, Paris, and London during their teens, the James children acquired languages and an awareness of Europe vouchsafed to few Americans in their times. On the eve of the American Civil War, the James family settled at Newport, R.I., and there, and later in Boston, Henry came to know New England intimately. When he was 19 years of age he enrolled at the Harvard Law School, but he devoted his study time to reading Charles-Augustin Sainte-Beuve, Honoré de Balzac, and Nathaniel Hawthorne. His first story appeared anonymously two years later in the New York *Continental Monthly* and his first book reviews in the *North American Review*. When William Dean Howells became editor of *The Atlantic Monthly,* James found in him a friend and mentor who published him regularly. Between them, James and Howells inaugurated the era of American "realism."

By his mid-20s James was regarded as one of the most skillful writers of short stories in America. Critics, however, deplored his tendency to write of the life of the mind, rather than of action. The stories of these early years show the leisurely existence of the well-to-do at Newport and Saratoga. James's apprenticeship was thorough. He wrote stories, reviews, and articles for almost a decade before he attempted a full-length novel. There had to be also the traditional "grand tour," and James went abroad for his first adult encounter with Europe in 1869. His year's wandering in England, France, and Italy set the stage for a lifetime of travel in those countries. James never married. By nature he was friendly and even gregarious, but while he was an active observer and participant in society, he tended, until late middle age, to be "distant" in his relations with people and was careful to avoid "involvement."

FIRST YEARS IN PARIS AND LONDON

Recognizing the appeal of Europe, given his cosmopolitan upbringing, James made a deliberate effort to discover whether he could live and work in the United States. Two years in Boston, two years in Europe, mainly in Rome, and a winter of unremitting hackwork in New York City convinced him that he could write better and live more cheaply abroad. Thus began his long expatriation—heralded by publication in 1875 of the novel *Roderick Hudson,* the story of an American sculptor's struggle by the banks of the Tiber between his art and his passions; *Transatlantic Sketches,* his first collection of travel writings; and a collection of tales. With these three substantial books, he inaugurated a career that saw about 100 volumes through the press during the next 40 years.

During 1875–76 James lived in Paris, writing literary and topical letters for the *New York Tribune* and working on his novel *The American* (1877), the story of a self-made

American millionaire whose guileless and forthright character contrasts with that of the arrogant and cunning family of French aristocrats whose daughter he unsuccessfully attempts to marry. In Paris James sought out the Russian novelist Ivan Turgenev, whose work appealed to him, and through Turgenev was brought into Gustave Flaubert's coterie, where he got to know Edmond de Goncourt, Émile Zola, Alphonse Daudet, and Guy de Maupassant. From Turgenev he received confirmation of his own view that a novelist need not worry about "story" and that, in focusing on character, he would arrive at the life experience of his protagonist.

Much as he liked France, James felt that he would be an eternal outsider there, and late in 1876 he crossed to London. There, in small rooms in Bolton Street off Piccadilly, he wrote the major fiction of his middle years. In 1878 he achieved international renown with his story of an American flirt in Rome, *Daisy Miller,* and further advanced his reputation with *The Europeans* that same year. In England he was promptly taken up by the leading Victorians and became a regular at Lord Houghton's breakfasts, where he consorted with Alfred Tennyson, William Gladstone, Robert Browning, and others. A great social lion, James dined out 140 times during 1878 and 1879 and visited in many of the great Victorian houses and country seats. He was elected to London clubs, published his stories simultaneously in English and American periodicals, and mingled with George Meredith, Robert Louis Stevenson, Edmund Gosse, and other writers, thus establishing himself as a significant figure in Anglo-American literary and artistic relations.

James's reputation was founded on his versatile studies of "the American girl." In a series of witty tales, he pictured the "self-made" young woman, the bold and brash

American innocent who insists upon American standards in European society. James ended this first phase of his career by producing his masterpiece, *The Portrait of a Lady* (1881), a study of a young woman from Albany who brings to Europe her narrow provincialism and pretensions but also her sense of her own sovereignty, her "free spirit," her refusal to be treated, in the Victorian world, merely as a marriageable object. As a picture of Americans moving in the expatriate society of England and of Italy, this novel has no equal in the history of modern fiction. It is a remarkable study of a band of egotists while at the same time offering a shrewd appraisal of the American character. James's understanding of power in personal relations was profound, as evinced in *Washington Square* (1881), the story of a young American heroine whose hopes for love and marriage are thwarted by her father's callous rejection of a somewhat opportunistic suitor.

THE "DRAMATIC YEARS"

In the 1880s James wrote two novels dealing with social reformers and revolutionaries, *The Bostonians* (1886) and *The Princess Casamassima* (1886). In the novel of Boston life, James analyzed the struggle between conservative masculinity embodied in a Southerner living in the North and an embittered man-hating suffragist. *The Bostonians* remains the fullest and most rounded American social novel of its time in its study of cranks, faddists, and "do-gooders." In *The Princess Casamassima* James exploited the anarchist violence of the decade and depicted the struggle of a man who toys with revolution and is destroyed by it. These novels were followed by *The Tragic Muse* (1890), in which James projected a study of the London and Paris art studios and the stage, the conflict between art and "the world."

The latter novel raised the curtain on his own "dramatic years," 1890–95, during which he tried to win success writing for the stage. His dramatization of *The American* in 1891 was a modest success, but an original play, *Guy Domville,* produced in 1895, was a failure, and James was booed at the end of the first performance. Crushed and feeling that he had lost his public, he spent several years seeking to adapt his dramatic experience to his fiction. The result was a complete change in his storytelling methods. In *The Spoils of Poynton* (1897), *What Maisie Knew* (1897), *The Turn of the Screw* and *In the Cage* (1898), and *The Awkward Age* (1899), James began to use the methods of alternating "picture" and dramatic scene, close adherence to a given angle of vision, a withholding of information from the reader, making available to him only that which the characters see. The subjects of this period are the developing consciousness and moral education of children—in reality James's old international theme of innocence in a corrupting world, transferred to the English setting.

THE "MAJOR PHASE"

The experiments of this "transition" phase led James to the writing of three grandiose novels at the beginning of the new century, which represent his final—his "major"—phase, as it has been called. In these novels James pointed the way for the 20th-century novel. He had begun as a realist who describes minutely his crowded stage. He ended by leaving his stage comparatively bare, and showing a small group of characters in a tense situation, with a retrospective working out, through multiple angles of vision, of their drama. In addition to these technical devices he resorted to an increasingly allusive prose style, which became dense and charged with symbolic

Henry James, at work in his study, began as a promising short story writer, segued into experimental tomes, and capped his career with works that laid the groundwork for modern novels. Hulton Archive/Getty Images

imagery. His late "manner" derived in part from his dictating directly to a typist and in part from his unremitting search for ways of projecting subjective experience in a flexible prose.

The first of the three novels was *The Ambassadors* (1903). This is a high comedy of manners, of a middle-aged American who goes to Paris to bring back to a Massachusetts industrial town a wealthy young man who, in the view of his affluent family, has lingered too long abroad. The "ambassador" in the end is captivated by civilized Parisian life. The novel is a study in the growth of perception and awareness in the elderly hero, and it balances the relaxed moral standards of the European continent against the parochial rigidities of New England. The second of this series of novels was *The Wings of the Dove,* published in 1902, before *The Ambassadors,* although written after it. This novel, dealing with a melodramatic subject of great pathos, that of an heiress doomed by illness to die, avoids its cliche subject by focusing upon the characters surrounding the unfortunate young woman. They intrigue to inherit her millions. Told in this way, and set in London and Venice, it becomes a powerful study of well-intentioned humans who, with dignity and reason, are at the same time also birds of prey. In its shifting points of view and avoidance of scenes that would end in melodrama, *The Wings of the Dove* demonstrated the mastery with which James could take a tawdry subject and invest it with grandeur. His final novel was *The Golden Bowl* (1904), a study of adultery, with four principal characters. The first part of the story is seen through the eyes of the aristocratic husband and the second through the developing awareness of the wife.

While many of James's short stories were potboilers written for the current magazines, he achieved high mastery in the ghostly form, notably in *The Turn of the Screw* (1898), and in such remarkable narratives as "The Aspern Papers" (1888) and "The Beast in the Jungle" (1903)—his prophetic picture of dissociated 20th-century man lost in an urban agglomeration. As a critic James tended to explore the character and personality of writers as revealed in their creations; his essays are a brilliant series of studies, moral portraits, of the most famous novelists of his century, from Balzac to the Edwardian realists. His travel writings, *English Hours* (1905), *Italian Hours* (1909), and *A Little Tour in France* (1884), portray the backgrounds James used for his fictions.

In his later years, James lived in retirement in an 18th-century house at Rye in Sussex, though on completion of *The Golden Bowl* he revisited the United States in 1904–05. James had lived abroad for 20 years, and in the interval America had become a great industrial and political power. His observation of the land and its people led him to write, on his return to England, a poetic volume of rediscovery and discovery, *The American Scene* (1907), prophetic in its vision of urban doom, spoliation, and pollution of resources and filled with misgivings over the anomalies of a "melting pot" civilization. The materialism of American life deeply troubled James, and on his return to England he set to work to shore up his own writings, and his own career, against this ephemeral world. He devoted three years to rewriting and revising his principal novels and tales for the highly selective "New York Edition," published in 24 volumes. For this edition James wrote 18 significant prefaces, which contain both reminiscence and exposition of his theories of fiction.

Throwing his moral weight into Britain's struggle in World War I, James became a British subject in 1915 and received the Order of Merit from King George V.

ASSESSMENT

Henry James's career was one of the longest and most productive—and most influential—in American letters. A master of prose fiction from the first, he practiced it as a fertile innovator, enlarged the form, and placed upon it the stamp of a highly individual method and style. He wrote for 51 years—20 novels, 112 tales, 12 plays, several volumes of travel and criticism, and a great deal of literary journalism. He recognized and helped to fashion the myth of the American abroad and incorporated this myth in the "international novel," of which he was the acknowledged master. His fundamental theme was that of an innocent, exuberant, and democratic America confronting the worldly wisdom and corruption of Europe's older, aristocratic culture. In both his light comedies and his tragedies,

James's sense of the human scene was sure and vivid; and, in spite of the mannerisms of his later style, he was one of the great prose writers and stylists of his century.

James's public remained limited during his lifetime, but, after a revival of interest in his work during the 1940s and '50s, he reached an ever-widening audience; his works were translated in many countries, and he was recognized in the late 20th century as one of the subtlest craftsmen who ever practiced the art of the novel. His rendering of the inner life of his characters made him a forerunner of the "stream-of-consciousness" movement in the 20th century.

JACK LONDON

(b. Jan. 12, 1876, San Francisco, Calif., U.S.—d. Nov. 22, 1916, Glen Ellen, Calif.)

Jack London was a novelist and short-story writer whose works deal romantically with elemental struggles for survival. He is one of the most extensively translated of American authors.

Deserted by his father, a roving astrologer, London was raised in Oakland, Calif., by his spiritualist mother and his stepfather, whose surname, London, he took. At 14 he quit school to escape poverty and gain adventure. He explored San Francisco Bay in his sloop, alternately stealing oysters or working for the government fish patrol. He went to Japan as a sailor and saw much of the United States as a hobo riding freight trains and as a member of Kelly's industrial army (one of the many protest armies of unemployed born of the panic of 1893). He saw depression conditions, was jailed for vagrancy, and in 1894 became a militant socialist. London educated himself at public libraries with the writings of Charles Darwin, Karl Marx, and Friedrich Nietzsche, usually in popularized forms,

Jack London writing The Sea Wolf, *1904.* Jack London State Historic Park

and created his own amalgam of socialism and white superiority. At 19 he crammed a four-year high school course into one year and entered the University of California at Berkeley, but after a year he quit school to seek a fortune in the Klondike gold rush of 1897. Returning the next year, still poor and unable to find work, he decided to earn a living as a writer.

London studied magazines and then set himself a daily schedule of producing sonnets, ballads, jokes, anecdotes, adventure stories, or horror stories, steadily increasing his output. The optimism and energy with which he attacked his task are best conveyed in his autobiographical novel *Martin Eden* (1909), perhaps his most enduring work. Within two years stories of his Alaskan adventures, though often crude, began to win acceptance for their fresh subject matter and virile force. His first book, *The Son of the Wolf* (1900), gained a wide audience. During the remainder of his life he produced steadily, completing 50 books of fiction and nonfiction in 17 years. Although he became the highest-paid writer in the United States, his earnings never matched his expenditures, and he was never freed of the urgency of writing for money. He sailed a ketch to the South Pacific, telling of his adventures in *The Cruise of the Snark* (1911). In 1910 he settled on a ranch near Glen Ellen, Calif., where he built his grandiose Wolf House. He maintained his socialist beliefs almost to the end of his life.

Jack London's hastily written output is of uneven quality. His Alaskan stories *Call of the Wild* (1903), *White Fang* (1906), and *Burning Daylight* (1910), in which he dramatized in turn atavism, adaptability, and the appeal of the wilderness, are outstanding. In addition to *Martin Eden,* he wrote two other autobiographical novels of considerable interest: *The Road* (1907) and *John Barleycorn* (1913). Other important works are *The Sea Wolf* (1904), which features a Nietzschean superman hero, and *The Iron Heel* (1907), a fantasy of the future that is a terrifying anticipation of fascism. London's reputation declined in the United States in the 1920s when a brilliant new generation of postwar writers made the prewar writers seem lacking in sophistication, but his popularity has remained high throughout the world, especially in Russia, where a commemorative edition of his works published in 1956 was reported to have been sold out in five hours. A three-volume set of his letters, edited by Earle Labor et al., was published in 1988.

EDITH WHARTON

(b. Jan. 24, 1862, New York, N.Y., U.S.—d. Aug. 11, 1937, St.-Brice-sous-Forêt, near Paris, France)

The American author Edith Wharton is best known for her stories and novels about the upper-class society into which she was born.

Edith Jones came from a distinguished and long-established New York family. She was educated by private tutors and governesses at home and in Europe, where the family resided for six years after the American Civil War, and she read voraciously. She made her debut in society in 1879 and married Edward Wharton, a wealthy Boston banker, in 1885.

Although she had had a book of her own poems privately printed when she was 16, it was not until after several years of married life that Wharton began to write in earnest. Her major literary model was Henry James, whom she knew, and her work reveals James's concern for artistic form and ethical issues. She contributed a few poems and stories to *Harper's, Scribner's,* and other magazines in the 1890s, and in 1897, after overseeing the remodeling of a house in Newport, R.I., she collaborated with the architect Ogden Codman, Jr., on *The Decoration of Houses.* Her next books, *The Greater Inclination* (1899) and *Crucial Instances* (1901), were collections of stories.

Author Edith Wharton wrote about the upper-class social circles in which she herself moved. Wharton is perhaps best known for The Age of Innocence, *which garnered her the Pulitzer Prize.* Hulton Archive/Getty Images

Wharton's first novel, *The Valley of Decision,* was published in 1902. *The House of Mirth* (1905) was a novel of manners that analyzed the stratified society in which she had been reared and its reaction to social change. The book won her critical acclaim and a wide audience. In the next two decades—before the quality of her work began to decline under the demands of writing for women's magazines—she wrote such novels as *The Reef* (1912), *The Custom of the Country* (1913), *Summer* (1917), and *The Age of Innocence* (1920), which won a Pulitzer Prize.

The Age of Innocence presents a picture of upper-class New York society in the 1870s. In the story, Newland Archer is engaged to May Welland, a beautiful but proper fellow member of elite society, but he falls deeply in love with Ellen Olenska, a former member of their circle who has returned to New York to escape her disastrous marriage to a Polish nobleman. Both lovers prove too obedient to conventional taboos to break with their upper-class social surroundings, however, and Newland feels compelled to renounce Ellen and marry May.

Wharton's best-known work is the long tale *Ethan Frome* (1911), which exploits the grimmer possibilities of the New England farm life she observed from her home in Lenox, Mass. The protagonist, the farmer Ethan Frome, is married to a whining hypochondriac but falls in love with her cousin, Mattie. As she is forced to leave his household, Frome tries to end their dilemma by steering their bobsled into a tree, but he ends up only crippling Mattie for life. They spend the rest of their miserable lives together with his wife on the farm.

Wharton's short stories, which appeared in numerous collections, among them *Xingu and Other Stories* (1916), demonstrate her gifts for social satire and comedy, as do the four novelettes collected in *Old New York* (1924). In her manual *The Writing of Fiction* (1925) she acknowledged her debt to Henry James. Among her later novels are *Twilight Sleep* (1927), *Hudson River Bracketed* (1929), and its sequel, *The Gods Arrive* (1932). Her autobiography, *A Backward Glance,* appeared in 1934. In all Wharton published more than 50 books, including fiction, short stories, travel books, historical novels, and criticism.

She lived in France after 1907, visiting the United States only at rare intervals. She was divorced from her husband in 1913 and was a close friend of novelist James in his later years.

CHAPTER 3

NOVELISTS AND SHORT-STORY WRITERS DURING THE WORLD WARS

Important movements in fiction took shape in the years before, during, and after World War I. The eventful period that followed the war left its imprint upon books of all kinds. Literary forms of the period were extraordinarily varied, and in fiction the leading authors tended toward radical technical experiments.

THE GROWTH OF MODERN FICTION

One of the more significant developments that spurred the experimentation in fiction at this time was the advent of the so-called little magazines in the late 19th century. They printed daring or unconventional short stories and published attacks upon established writers. *The Dial* (1880–1929), *Little Review* (1914–29), *Seven Arts* (1916–17), and others encouraged Modernist innovation. One of the most influential of the avant-garde writers whose work was published in the little magazines was Gertrude Stein. Her novels, short stories, and plays, with their stripped down and distorted language, led to a remarkable critical reputation, but she is probably best remembered for her most conventional work, *The Autobiography of Alice B. Toklas* (1933).

Little Magazine

A little magazine was any of various small periodicals devoted to serious literary writings, usually avant-garde and noncommercial. They were published from about 1880 through much of the 20th century and flourished in the United States and England, though French writers (especially the Symbolist poets and critics, 1880–*c*. 1900) often had access to a similar type of publication and German literature of the 1920s was also indebted to them. The name signifies most of all a noncommercial manner of editing, managing, and financing. A little magazine usually begins with the object of publishing literary work of some artistic merit that is unacceptable to commercial magazines for any one or all of three reasons—the writer is unknown and therefore not a good risk; the work itself is unconventional or experimental in form; or it violates one of several popular notions of moral, social, or aesthetic behaviour.

Foremost in the ranks of such magazines were two American periodicals, *Poetry: a Magazine of Verse* (founded 1912), especially in its early years under the vigorous guidance of Harriet Monroe, and the more erratic and often more sensational *Little Review* (1914–29) of Margaret Anderson; a group of English magazines in the second decade of the 20th century, of which the *Egoist* (1914–19) and *Blast* (1914–15) were most conspicuous; and Eugene Jolas' *transition* (1927–38). In all but the last of these, a major guiding spirit was the U.S. poet and critic Ezra Pound; he served as "foreign correspondent" of both *Poetry* and the *Little Review,* maneuvred the *Egoist* from its earlier beginnings as a feminist magazine (*The New Freewoman,* 1913) to the status of an avant-garde literary review, and, with Wyndham Lewis, jointly sponsored the two issues of *Blast.* In this case, the little magazines showed the stamp of a single vigorous personality; similar strong and dedicated figures in little magazine history were the U.S. poet William Carlos Williams (whose name appears in scores of little magazines, in one capacity or another); the British critic and novelist Ford Madox Ford, editor of the *Transatlantic Review* (1924–25) and contributor to many others; and Gustave Kahn, a minor French poet but a very active editor associated with several French Symbolist periodicals.

There were four principal periods in the general history of little magazines. In the first, from 1890 to about 1915, French magazines served mainly to establish and explain a literary movement; British and U.S. magazines served to disseminate information about and encourage acceptance of continental European literature and culture. In the second stage, 1915–30, when other magazines, especially in the United States, were in the vanguard of almost every variation of modern literature, a conspicuous feature was the expatriate magazine, published usually in France but occasionally elsewhere in Europe by young U.S. and British critics and writers. The major emphasis in this period was upon literary and aesthetic form and theory and the publication of fresh and original work, such as that of Ernest Hemingway (in the *Little Review, Poetry, This Quarter,* and other publications), T.S. Eliot (in *Poetry,* the *Egoist, Blast*) James Joyce (in the *Egoist,* the *Little Review, transition*), and many others. The third stage, the 1930s, saw the beginnings of many leftist magazines, started with specific doctrinal commitments that were often subjected to considerable editorial change in the career of the magazine. *Partisan Review* (1934) was perhaps the best known example of these in the United States, as was the *Left Review* (1934–38) in England.

The fourth period of little magazine history began about 1940. One of the conspicuous features of this period was the critical review supported and sustained by a group of critics, who were in most cases attached to a university or college. Examples of this kind of periodical were, in the United States, *The Kenyon Review,* founded by John Crowe Ransom in 1939, and in Great Britain, *Scrutiny,* edited by F.R. Leavis (1932–53). This and related kinds of support, such as that of publishers maintaining their own reviews or miscellanies, represented a form of institutionalism which was radically different from the more spontaneous and erratic nature of the little magazines of earlier years.

More potent than the little magazines were two magazines edited by the ferociously funny journalist-critic H.L. Mencken—*The Smart Set* (editorship 1914–23) and *American Mercury* (which he coedited between 1924 and 1933). A powerful influence and a scathing critic of puritanism,

Mencken helped launch the new fiction. His major enthusiasms included the fiction of Joseph Conrad and Theodore Dreiser, but he also promoted minor writers for their attacks on gentility, such as James Branch Cabell, or their revolt against the narrow, frustrated quality of life in rural communities, including Zona Gale and Ruth Suckow. The most distinguished of these writers was Sherwood Anderson. His *Winesburg, Ohio* (1919) and *The Triumph of the Egg* (1921) were collections of short stories that showed villagers suffering from all sorts of phobias and suppressions. Anderson in time wrote several novels. Among the best was *Poor White* (1920).

Rural life abroad, specifically the plight of peasants in China, was explored by Nobel Prize-winner (1938) Pearl Buck. Her novels were tremendously popular and greatly increased awareness of Chinese culture in the Western world. A writer concerned with the opposite end of the cultural spectrum was Dorothy Parker, whose witty short stories often revolved around the goings-on of upper-crust New Yorkers. Parker's work was included in both mainstream and little magazines, and she gained a good measure of nonliterary fame from her many epigrammatic aphorisms.

GERTRUDE STEIN

(b. Feb. 3, 1874, Allegheny City, now in Pittsburgh, Pa., U.S.—d. July 27, 1946, Neuilly-sur-Seine, France)

Gertrude Stein was an avant-garde American writer and self-styled genius whose Paris home was a salon for the leading artists and writers of the period between World Wars I and II.

Stein spent her infancy in Vienna and in Passy, France, and her girlhood in Oakland, Calif. She entered the Society for the Collegiate Instruction of Women (renamed Radcliffe College in 1894), where she studied psychology with the philosopher William James, and received her degree in 1898. She studied at Johns Hopkins Medical School from 1897 to 1902 and then, with her older brother Leo, moved first to London and then to Paris, where she was able to live by private means. She lived with Leo, who became an accomplished art critic, until 1909; thereafter she lived with her lifelong companion Alice B. Toklas (1877–1967).

Stein and her brother were among the first collectors of works by the Cubists and other experimental painters of the period, such as Pablo Picasso (who painted her portrait), Henri Matisse, and Georges Braque, several of whom became her friends. At her salon they mingled with expatriate American writers whom she dubbed the "Lost Generation," including Sherwood Anderson and Ernest Hemingway, and other visitors drawn by her literary reputation. Her literary and artistic judgments were revered, and her chance remarks could make or destroy reputations.

In her own work, she attempted to parallel the theories of Cubism, specifically in her concentration on the illumination of the present moment (for which she often relied on the present perfect tense) and her use of slightly varied repetitions and extreme simplification and fragmentation. The best explanation of her theory of writing is found in the essay *Composition and Explanation*, which is based on lectures that she gave at the Universities of Oxford and Cambridge and was issued as a book in 1926. Among her work that was most thoroughly influenced by Cubism is *Tender Buttons* (1914), which carries fragmentation and abstraction to an extreme.

Her first published book, *Three Lives* (1909), the stories of three working-class women, has been called a minor masterpiece. *The Making of Americans,* a long composition written in 1906–11 but not published until 1925, was too convoluted and obscure for general readers, for whom she remained essentially the author of such lines as "Rose is a rose is a rose is a rose." Her only book to reach a wide public was *The Autobiography of Alice B. Toklas* (1933), actually Stein's own autobiography. The performance in the United States of her *Four Saints in Three Acts* (1934), which the composer Virgil Thomson had made into an opera, led to a triumphal American lecture tour in 1934–35. Thomson also wrote the music for her second opera, *The Mother of Us All* (published 1947), based on the life of feminist Susan B. Anthony. One of Stein's early short stories, "Q.E.D.," was first published in *Things as They Are* (1950).

The eccentric Stein was not modest in her self-estimation: "Einstein was the creative philosophic mind of the century, and I have been the creative literary mind of the century." She became a legend in Paris, especially after surviving the German occupation of France and befriending the many young American servicemen who visited her. She wrote about these soldiers in *Brewsie and Willie* (1946).

H.L. MENCKEN
(b. Sept. 12, 1880, Baltimore, Md., U.S.—d. Jan. 29, 1956, Baltimore)

H.L. Mencken was a controversialist, humorous journalist, and pungent critic of American life who powerfully influenced U.S. fiction through the 1920s.

Henry Louis Mencken attended a Baltimore private school and the Baltimore Polytechnic. He became a reporter for the *Baltimore Morning Herald* in 1899 and in 1906 joined the staff of the Baltimore *Sun,* where he worked at intervals throughout most of his life. From 1914

H.L. Mencken. Enoch Pratt Free Library, Baltimore; photograph, Robert Kniesche

to 1923 he coedited (with George Jean Nathan) *The Smart Set,* a witty, urban magazine influential in the growth of American literature, and in 1924 he and Nathan founded the *American Mercury,* which Mencken edited until 1933.

Mencken was probably the most influential American literary critic in the 1920s, and he often used his criticism as a point of departure to jab at various American social and cultural weaknesses. His reviews and miscellaneous essays filled six volumes aptly titled *Prejudices* (1919–27). In literature he fought against what he regarded as fraudulently successful writers and worked for the recognition of such outstanding newcomers as Theodore Dreiser and Sinclair Lewis. He jeered at American sham, pretension, provincialism, and prudery, and he ridiculed the nation's organized religion, business, and middle class (or "booboisie").

Mencken's caustic view of life remained with him throughout his career, and in the 1930s and '40s he altered considerably less than the world around him, with the result that his influence almost disappeared. Few people found the Great Depression a subject for satire of any sort, yet he was as satirical about President Franklin D. Roosevelt and the New Deal as he had been about President Herbert Hoover and Prohibition. Similarly, when the German culture that he had enjoyed was marred by Adolf Hitler and Nazism, Mencken was slower than some of his public to recognize it and to take the fact seriously.

Mencken made still another contribution to American culture. In 1919 he had published a solid volume, *The American Language*, an attempt to bring together examples of American, rather than English, expressions and idioms. The book at once attracted attention. It grew with each reissue through the years, and in 1945 and 1948 Mencken published substantial supplements. By the time of his death, he was perhaps the leading authority on the language of his country.

Mencken's autobiographical trilogy, *Happy Days* (1940), *Newspaper Days* (1941), and *Heathen Days* (1943), is devoted to his experiences in journalism.

SHERWOOD ANDERSON

(b. Sept. 13, 1876, Camden, Ohio, U.S.—d. March 8, 1941, Colon, Panama)

The American author Sherwood Anderson strongly influenced American writing between World Wars I and II, particularly the technique of the short story. His writing had an impact on such notable writers as Ernest Hemingway and William Faulkner, both of whom owe the first publication of their books to his efforts. His prose style, based on everyday speech and derived from the experimental writing of Gertrude Stein, was markedly influential on the early Hemingway—who parodied it cruelly in *Torrents of Spring* (1926) to make a clean break and become his own man.

One of seven children of a day labourer, Anderson attended school intermittently as a youth in Clyde, Ohio, and worked as a newsboy, house painter, farmhand, and racetrack helper. After a year at Wittenberg Academy, a preparatory school in Springfield, Ohio, he worked as an advertising writer in Chicago until 1906, when he went back to Ohio and for the next six years sought without success—to prosper as a businessman while writing fiction in his spare time. A paint manufacturer in Elyria, Ohio, he left his office abruptly one day in 1912 and wandered off, turning up four days later in Cleveland, disheveled and mentally distraught. He later said he staged this episode to get away from the business world and devote himself to literature.

Anderson went back to his advertising job in Chicago and remained there until he began to earn enough from his published work to quit. Encouraged by Dreiser, Floyd Dell, Carl Sandburg, and Ben Hecht—leaders of the Chicago literary movement—he began to contribute experimental verse and short fiction to *Little Review,* *The Masses,* the *Seven Arts,* and *Poetry.* Dell and Dreiser arranged the publication of his first two novels, *Windy McPherson's Son* (1916; rev. 1921) and *Marching Men* (1917), both written while he was still a manufacturer. *Winesburg, Ohio* (1919) was his first mature book and made his reputation as an author. Its interrelated short sketches and tales are told by a newspaper reporter-narrator who is as emotionally stunted in some ways as the people he describes. His novels include *Many Marriages* (1923), which stresses the need for sexual fulfillment; *Dark Laughter* (1925), which values the "primitive" over the civilized; and *Beyond Desire* (1932), a novel of Southern textile mill labour struggles.

His best work is generally thought to be in his short stories, collected in *Winesburg, Ohio, The Triumph of the Egg* (1921), *Horses and Men* (1923), and *Death in the Woods* (1933). Also valued are the autobiographical sketches *A Story Teller's Story* (1924), *Tar: A Midwest Childhood* (1926), and the posthumous *Memoirs* (1942; critical edition 1969). A selection of his letters appeared in 1953.

PEARL BUCK

(b. June 26, 1892, Hillsboro, W.Va., U.S.—d. March 6, 1973, Danby, Vt.)

Author Pearl Buck is noted for her novels of life in China. She received the Nobel Prize for Literature in 1938.

Pearl Sydenstricker was raised in Chenchiang in eastern China by her Presbyterian missionary parents. Initially educated by her mother and a Chinese tutor, she was sent at 15 to a boarding school in Shanghai. Two years later she entered Randolph-Macon Woman's College in Lynchburg, Virginia, graduating in 1914 and remaining for a semester as an instructor in psychology.

In May 1917 she married missionary John L. Buck; although later divorced and remarried, she retained the name Buck professionally. She returned to China and taught English literature in Chinese universities in 1925–30. During that time she briefly resumed studying in the United States at Cornell University, where she took her M.A. in 1926. She began contributing articles on Chinese life to American magazines in 1922.

Buck's first published novel, *East Wind, West Wind* (1930), was written aboard a ship headed for America. *The Good Earth* (1931), a poignant tale of a Chinese peasant and his slave-wife and their struggle upward, was a best-seller. The book, which won a Pulitzer Prize (1932), established Buck as an interpreter of the East to the West and was adapted for stage and screen. *The Good Earth*, widely translated, was followed by *Sons* (1932) and *A House Divided* (1935); the trilogy was published as *The House of Earth* (1935). She was awarded the Nobel Prize for Literature in 1938.

From 1935 Buck lived in the United States. After World War II, in a move to aid illegitimate children of U.S. servicemen in Asian countries, she instituted the Pearl S. Buck Foundation. In 1967 she turned over to the foundation most of her earnings, more than $7 million.

Buck turned next to biography with lives of her father, Absalom Sydenstricker, *Fighting Angel* (1936), and her mother, Caroline, *The Exile* (1936). Her later novels include *Dragon Seed* (1942) and *Imperial Woman* (1956). She also published short stories, such as *The First Wife and Other Stories . . .* (1933), *Far and Near* (1947), and *The Good Deed* (1969); a nonfictional work, *The Child Who Never Grew* (1950), about her developmentally disabled daughter; and three works of autobiography, notably *My Several Worlds* (1954). She also wrote a number of children's books. Under the name John Sedges she published five novels unlike her others, including a best-seller, *The Townsman* (1945).

DOROTHY PARKER

(b. Aug. 22, 1893, West End, near Long Beach, N.J., U.S.—d. June 7, 1967, New York, N.Y.)

The American short-story writer and poet Dorothy Parker is known for her witty remarks and her role in helping found the literary group known as the Algonquin Round Table.

Dorothy Rothschild was educated at Miss Dana's School in Morristown, N.J., and the Blessed Sacrament Convent School, New York City. She joined the editorial staff of *Vogue* magazine in 1916 and the next year moved to *Vanity Fair* as a drama critic. In 1917 she married Edwin Pond Parker II, whom she divorced in 1928 but whose surname she retained in her professional career.

Discharged from *Vanity Fair* in 1920 for the acerbity of her drama reviews, she became a freelance writer. Her first book of light, witty, and sometimes cynical verse, *Enough Rope,* was a best-seller when it appeared in 1926. Two other books of verse, *Sunset Gun* (1928) and *Death and Taxes* (1931), were collected with it in *Collected Poems: Not So Deep as a Well* (1936). In 1927 Parker became book reviewer, known as "Constant Reader," for *The New Yorker,* and she was associated with that magazine as a staff writer or contributor for much of the rest of her career.

Early in the 1920s she had been one of the founders of the famous Algonquin Round Table at the Algonquin Hotel in Manhattan and was by no means the least of a group of dazzling wits that included Robert Benchley, Robert E. Sherwood, and James Thurber. It was there, in conversations that frequently spilled over from the offices

Dorothy Parker, 1939. Culver Pictures

of *The New Yorker,* that Parker established her reputation as one of the most brilliant conversationalists in New York. Her rapier wit became so widely renowned that quips and mots were frequently attributed to her on the strength of her reputation alone. She came to epitomize the liberated woman of the 1920s.

In 1929 Parker won the O. Henry Award for the best short story of the year with "Big Blonde," a compassionate account of an aging party girl. *Laments for the Living* (1930) and *After Such Pleasures* (1933) are collections of her short stories, combined and augmented in 1939 as *Here Lies.* Characteristic of both the stories and Parker's verses is a view of the human situation as simultaneously tragic and funny.

In 1933, the newly married Parker and her second husband, Alan Campbell, went to Hollywood to collaborate as film writers, receiving screen credits for more than 15 films, including *A Star Is Born* (1937), for which they were nominated for an Academy Award. She became active in left-wing politics, disdained her former role as a smart woman about town, reported from the Spanish Civil War, and discovered that her beliefs counted against her employment by the studios in the fervour of anticommunism that seized Hollywood after World War II. She wrote book reviews for *Esquire* magazine and collaborated on two plays: *The Coast of Illyria* (first performance 1949), about the English essayist Charles Lamb, and *The Ladies of the Corridor* (1953), about lonely widows in side-street New York hotels.

Parker's witty remarks are legendary. When told of the death of the taciturn U.S. president Calvin Coolidge, she is said to have asked, "How can they tell?" Of Katharine Hepburn's performance in a 1934 play, Parker said she "ran the gamut of emotions from A to B." She also is responsible for the couplet "Men seldom make passes / at girls who wear glasses." She lived in Hollywood until Campbell's death in 1963 and then returned to New York City.

CRITICS OF SOCIETY

In 1920 critics noticed that a new school of fiction had risen to prominence with the success of books such as F. Scott Fitzgerald's *This Side of Paradise* and Sinclair Lewis's *Main Street*, fictions that tended to be frankly psychological or modern in their unsparing portrayals of contemporary life. Novels of the 1920s were often not only lyrical and personal but also, in the despairing mood that followed World War I, apt to express the pervasive disillusionment of the postwar generation. Novels of the 1930s inclined toward radical social criticism in response to the miseries of the Great Depression, though some of the best, by writers such as Fitzgerald, William Faulkner, Henry Roth, and Nathanael West, continued to explore the Modernist vein of the previous decade.

Fitzgerald's *This Side of Paradise* (1920) showed the disillusionment and moral disintegration experienced by so many in the United States after World War I. The book initiated a career of great promise that found fruition in *The Great Gatsby* (1925), a spare but poignant novel about

Algonquin Round Table

The Algonquin Round Table, also called the Round Table, was an informal group of American literary men and women who met daily for lunch on weekdays at a large round table in the Algonquin Hotel in New York City during the 1920s and '30s. The Algonquin Round Table began meeting in 1919, and within a few years its participants included many of the best-known writers, journalists, and artists in New York City. Among them were Dorothy Parker, Alexander Woollcott, Heywood Broun, Robert Benchley, Robert Sherwood, George S. Kaufman, Franklin P. Adams, Marc Connelly, Harold Ross, Harpo Marx, and Russell Crouse. The Round Table became celebrated in the 1920s for its members' lively, witty conversation and urbane sophistication. Its members gradually went their separate ways, however, and the last meeting of the Round Table took place in 1943.

the promise and failure of the American Dream. Fitzgerald was to live out this theme himself. Though damaged by drink and by a failing marriage, he went on to do some of his best work in the 1930s, including numerous stories and essays as well as his most ambitious novel, *Tender Is the Night* (1934). Unlike Fitzgerald, who was a lyric writer with real emotional intensity, Sinclair Lewis was best as a social critic. His onslaughts against the "village virus" (*Main Street* [1920]), average businessmen (*Babbitt* [1922]), materialistic scientists (*Arrowsmith* [1925]), and the racially prejudiced (*Kingsblood Royal* [1947]) were satirically sharp and thoroughly documented, though *Babbitt* is his only book that still stands up brilliantly at the beginning of the 21st century. Similar careful documentation, though little satire, characterized James T. Farrell's naturalistic *Studs Lonigan* trilogy (1932–35), which described the stifling effects of growing up in a lower-middle-class family and a street-corner milieu in the Chicago of the 1920s.

A number of authors wrote proletarian novels attacking capitalist exploitation, as in several novels based on a 1929 strike in the textile mills in Gastonia, N.C., such as Fielding Burke's *Call Home the Heart* and Grace Lumpkin's *To Make My Bread* (both 1932). Other notable proletarian novels included Jack Conroy's *The Disinherited* (1933), Robert Cantwell's *The Land of Plenty* (1934), and Albert Halper's *Union Square* (1933), *The Foundry* (1934), and *The Chute* (1937), as well as some grim evocations of the drifters and "bottom dogs" of the Depression era, such as Edward Anderson's *Hungry Men* and Tom Kromer's *Waiting for Nothing* (both 1935). The radical movement, combined with a nascent feminism, encouraged the talent of several politically committed women writers whose work was rediscovered later; they included Tillie Olsen, Meridel Le Sueur, and Josephine Herbst.

Particularly admired as a protest writer was John Dos Passos, who first attracted attention with an anti-World War I novel, *Three Soldiers* (1921). His most sweeping indictments of the modern social and economic system, *Manhattan Transfer* (1925) and the *U.S.A.* trilogy (*The 42nd Parallel*, *1919*, and *The Big Money* [1930–36]), employed various narrative innovations such as the "camera eye" and "newsreel," along with a large cast of characters, to attack society from the left. Nathanael West's novels, including *Miss Lonelyhearts* (1933), *A Cool Million* (1934), and *The Day of the Locust* (1939), used black comedy to create a bitter vision of an inhuman and brutal world and its depressing effects on his sensitive but ineffectual protagonists. West evoked the tawdry but rich materials of mass culture and popular fantasy to mock the pathos of the American Dream, a frequent target during the Depression years.

F. SCOTT FITZGERALD

(b. Sept. 24, 1896, St. Paul,
Minn., U.S.—d. Dec. 21, 1940,
Hollywood, Calif.)

F. Scott Fitzgerald.

The short-story writer and novelist F. Scott Fitzgerald is famous for his depictions of the Jazz Age (the 1920s), his most brilliant novel being *The Great Gatsby* (1925). His private life, with his wife, Zelda, in both America and France, became almost as celebrated as his novels.

Francis Scott Key Fitzgerald was the only son of an unsuccessful, aristocratic father and an energetic, provincial mother. Half the time he thought of himself as the heir of his father's tradition, which included the author of "The Star-Spangled Banner," Francis Scott Key, after whom he was named, and half the time as "straight 1850 potato-famine Irish." As a result he had typically ambivalent American feelings about American life, which seemed to him at once vulgar and dazzlingly promising.

He also had an intensely romantic imagination, what he once called "a heightened sensitivity to the promises of life." He charged into experience determined to realize those promises. At both St. Paul Academy (1908–10) and Newman School (1911–13) he tried too hard and made himself unpopular, but at Princeton he came close to realizing his dream of a brilliant success. He became a prominent figure in the literary life of the university and made lifelong friendships with Edmund Wilson and John Peale Bishop. He became a leading figure in the socially important Triangle Club, a dramatic society, and was elected to one of the leading clubs of the university. Fitzgerald fell in love with Ginevra King, one of the beauties of her generation, but then lost her and flunked out of Princeton.

He returned to Princeton the next fall, but he had now lost all the positions he coveted, and in November 1917 he left to join the army. In July 1918, while he was stationed near Montgomery, Ala., he met Zelda Sayre, the daughter of an Alabama Supreme Court judge. They fell deeply in love, and, as soon as he could, Fitzgerald headed for New York determined to achieve instant success and to marry Zelda. What he achieved was an advertising job at $90 a month. Zelda broke their engagement, and, after an epic drunk, Fitzgerald retired to St. Paul to rewrite for the second time a novel he had begun at Princeton. In the spring of 1920 it was published, he married Zelda, and

> *riding in a taxi one afternoon between very tall buildings under a mauve and rosy sky; I began to bawl because I had everything I wanted and knew I would never be so happy again.*

Immature though it may seem today, *This Side of Paradise* in 1920 was a revelation of the new morality of the young; it made Fitzgerald famous. This fame opened to him magazines of literary prestige, such as *Scribner's,* and high-paying popular ones, such as *The Saturday Evening Post.* This sudden prosperity made it possible for him and Zelda to play the roles they were so beautifully equipped for, and Ring Lardner called them the prince and princess of their generation. Though they loved these roles, they were frightened by them, too, as the ending of Fitzgerald's second novel shows. *The Beautiful and Damned* (1922) describes a handsome young man and his beautiful wife, who gradually degenerate into a shopworn middle age while they wait for the young man to inherit a large fortune. Ironically, they finally get it, when there is nothing of them left worth preserving.

To escape the life that they feared might bring them to this end, the Fitzgeralds (together with their daughter, Frances, called "Scottie," born in 1921) moved in 1924 to the Riviera, where they found themselves a part of a group of American expatriates whose style was largely set by Gerald and Sara Murphy; Fitzgerald described this society in his last completed novel, *Tender Is the Night,* and modeled its hero on Gerald Murphy. Shortly after their arrival in France, Fitzgerald completed his most brilliant novel, *The Great Gatsby* (1925). All of his divided nature is in this novel, the naive Midwesterner afire with the possibilities of the "American Dream" in its hero, Jay Gatsby, and the compassionate Princeton gentleman in its narrator, Nick Carraway. *The Great Gatsby* is the most profoundly American novel of its time; at its conclusion, Fitzgerald connects Gatsby's dream, his "Platonic conception of himself," with the dream of the discoverers of America. Some of Fitzgerald's finest short stories appeared in *All the Sad Young Men* (1926), particularly "The Rich Boy" and "Absolution," but it was not until eight years later that another novel appeared.

The next decade of the Fitzgeralds' lives was disorderly and unhappy. Fitzgerald began to drink too much, and Zelda suddenly, ominously, began to practice ballet dancing night and day. In 1930 she had a mental breakdown and in 1932 another, from which she never fully recovered. Through the 1930s they fought to save their life together, and, when the battle was lost, Fitzgerald said, "I left my capacity for hoping on the little roads that led to Zelda's sanitarium." He did not finish his next novel, *Tender Is the Night,* until 1934. It is the story of a psychiatrist who marries one of his patients, who, as she slowly recovers, exhausts his vitality until he is, in Fitzgerald's words, *un homme épuisé* ("a man used up"). Though technically faulty and commercially unsuccessful, this is Fitzgerald's most moving book.

With its failure and his despair over Zelda, Fitzgerald was close to becoming an incurable alcoholic. By 1937, however, he had come back far enough to become a scriptwriter in Hollywood, and there he met and fell in love with Sheilah Graham, a famous Hollywood gossip columnist. For the rest of his life—except for occasional drunken spells when he became bitter and violent—Fitzgerald lived quietly with her. (Occasionally he went east to visit Zelda or his daughter Scottie, who entered Vassar College in 1938.) In October 1939 he began a novel about Hollywood, *The Last Tycoon*. The career of its hero, Monroe Stahr, is based on that of the producer Irving Thalberg. This is Fitzgerald's final attempt to create his dream of the promises of American life and of the kind of man who could realize them. In the intensity with which it is imagined and in the brilliance of its expression, it is the equal of anything Fitzgerald ever wrote, and it is typical of his luck that he died of a heart attack with his novel only half-finished. He was 44 years old.

SINCLAIR LEWIS
(b. Feb. 7, 1885, Sauk Centre, Minn., U.S.—d. Jan. 10, 1951, near Rome, Italy)

The novelist and social critic Sinclair Lewis punctured American complacency with his broadly drawn, widely popular satirical novels. He won the Nobel Prize for Literature in 1930, the first given to an American.

Lewis graduated from Yale University (1907) and was for a time a reporter and also worked as an editor for several publishers. His first novel, *Our Mr. Wrenn* (1914), attracted favourable criticism but few readers. At the same time he was writing with ever-increasing success for such popular magazines as *The Saturday Evening Post* and *Cosmopolitan,* but he never lost sight of his ambition to become a serious novelist. He undertook the writing of *Main Street* as a major effort, assuming that it would not bring him the ready rewards of magazine fiction. Yet its publication in 1920 made his literary reputation.

Main Street is seen through the eyes of Carol Kennicott, an Eastern girl married to a Midwestern doctor who settles in Gopher Prairie, Minn. (modeled on Lewis's hometown of Sauk Centre). The power of the book derives from Lewis's careful rendering of local speech, customs, and social amenities. The satire is double-edged—directed against both the townspeople and the superficial intellectualism that despises them. In the years following its publication, *Main Street* became not just a novel but the textbook on American provincialism.

In 1922 Lewis published *Babbitt,* a study of the complacent American whose individuality has been sucked out of him by Rotary clubs, business ideals, and general conformity. The name Babbitt passed into general usage to represent the optimistic, self-congratulatory, middle-aged businessman whose horizons were bounded by his village limits.

He followed this success with *Arrowsmith* (1925), a satiric study of the medical profession, with emphasis on the frustration of fine scientific ideals. His next important book, *Elmer Gantry* (1927), was an attack on the ignorant, gross, and predatory leaders who had crept into the Protestant church. *Dodsworth* (1929), concerning the experiences of a retired big businessman and his wife on a European tour, offered Lewis a chance to contrast American and European values and the very different temperaments of the man and his wife.

Lewis's later books were not up to the standards of his work in the 1920s. *It Can't Happen Here* (1935) dramatized the possibilities of a Fascist takeover of the United States. It was produced as a play by the Federal Theatre with 21 companies in 1936. *Kingsblood Royal* (1947) is a novel of race relations.

In his final years Lewis lived much of the time abroad. His reputation declined steadily after 1930. His two marriages (the second was to the political columnist Dorothy Thompson) ended in divorce, and he drank excessively.

JAMES T. FARRELL

(b. Feb. 27, 1904, Chicago, Ill., U.S.—d. Aug. 22, 1979, New York, N.Y.)

James T. Farrell was an American novelist and short-story writer known for his realistic portraits of the lower-middle-class Irish in Chicago, drawn from his own experiences.

Farrell belonged to a working-class Irish American family. His impoverished parents gave Farrell over to be raised by middle-class relatives. Financing himself by working at various jobs, including gas-station attendant, Farrell attended the University of Chicago from 1925 to 1929. He began to write seriously about 1925, shaping his writing to reveal his conviction that destinies are shaped by environment. He left the university before graduating, determined to become a writer.

In 1931 he went to Paris with a young woman. The next year he settled down in New York City and published the first volume of his well-known *Studs Lonigan* trilogy, *Young Lonigan*. It was followed by *The Young Manhood of Studs Lonigan* in 1934 and *Judgment Day* in 1935. The series traces the self-destruction of a young man who has been spiritually crippled by the morally squalid urban environment in which he lives. Danny O'Neill, a character introduced in *Studs Lonigan*, is the subject of a later series

(1936–53), in which he reflects Farrell's acquired faith in humanitarian values and man's power to cope with circumstances. Of this series the volume *The Face of Time* (1953) is considered one of Farrell's best works.

Farrell's relentless and rather humourless naturalism led some critics to suggest that his works are only shocking and highly detailed case histories; his fiction is nevertheless durable in its deep understanding of the lower-middle-class mentalities it describes.

After 1958 Farrell worked on what was to be a 25-volume cycle, *A Universe of Time*, of which he completed 10 volumes. His complete works include 25 novels and 17 collections of short stories. Among his works of nonfiction are *A Note on Literary Criticism* (1936), a discussion of Marxist literature, and *Reflections at Fifty* (1954), personal essays.

TILLIE OLSEN

(b. Jan. 14, 1913?, Omaha, Neb., U.S.—d. Jan. 1, 2007, Oakland, Calif.)

Tillie Olsen was an American author known for her powerful fiction about the inner lives of the working poor, women, and minorities.

Tillie Lerner was born to Russian immigrants who instilled in their daughter a strong commitment to social activism from a young age. She joined a series of leftist groups as a teenager, and she was arrested for trying to organize workers in Kansas City, Mo., in 1932. Lerner moved to San Francisco in 1933 and continued her political involvement, which led to a second arrest for participating in a protest march after the citywide general strike in 1934. She reported on the strike and its aftermath for *The Partisan Review*, her first published work. In 1937 she began living with a union printer named Jack Olsen, whom she married in 1943.

Olsen's first novel, begun at the age of 19, was set aside for 35 years. Though she never finished it, Olsen eventually published the reconstructed manuscript as *Yonnondio: From the Thirties* in 1974. It tells the story of the Holbrook family, who struggle to survive the Great Depression, working as coal miners, tenant farmers, and meat packers, and who finally give in to despair. Olsen's best-known work is *Tell Me a Riddle: A Collection* (1961), a volume of three short stories and a novella, each a masterpiece in its own right. "Tell Me a Riddle" is the story of a quarreling old Jewish couple who, while the wife is dying of cancer, remember their youth of political activism, their disappointments in marriage, and the various compromises they have been forced to make in their lives. The protagonist in "I Stand Here Ironing" is a mother who realizes that, because of the deadening effects of poverty, her 19-year-old daughter will never be able to develop fully as a human being. Olsen used rhythmic, metaphoric language to give a voice to otherwise inarticulate characters. Her stories capture the tragedy of their lives with poignant clarity.

In her later works Olsen addressed feminist themes and concerns, especially as related to women writers. *Silences* (1978) contains, among other things, a long essay about the author Rebecca Harding Davis, whose career as a writer failed after she married. In 1984 she edited *Mother to Daughter, Daughter to Mother: Mothers on Mothering*.

JOHN DOS PASSOS

(b. Jan. 14, 1896, Chicago, Ill., U.S.—d. Sept. 28, 1970, Baltimore, Md.)

The American writer John Dos Passos was one of the major novelists of the post-World War I "lost generation," whose reputation as a social historian and as a radical critic

John Dos Passos. Library of Congress Prints and Photographs Division

of the quality of American life rests primarily on his trilogy *U.S.A.*

The son of a wealthy lawyer of Portuguese descent, Dos Passos graduated from Harvard University (1916) and volunteered as an ambulance driver in World War I. His early works were basically portraits of the artist recoiling from the shock of his encounter with a brutal world. Among these was the bitter antiwar novel *Three Soldiers* (1921).

Extensive travel in Spain and other countries while working as a newspaper correspondent in the postwar years enlarged his sense of history, sharpened his social perception, and confirmed his radical sympathies. Gradually, his early subjectivism was subordinated to a larger and tougher objective realism. His novel *Manhattan Transfer* (1925) is a rapid-transit rider's view of the metropolis. The narrative shuttles back and forth between the lives of more than a dozen characters in nervous, jerky, impressionistic flashes.

The execution of the Anarchists Nicola Sacco and Bartolomeo Vanzetti in 1927 profoundly affected Dos Passos, who had participated in the losing battle to win their pardon. The crisis crystallized his image of the United States as "two nations"—one of the rich and privileged and one of the poor and powerless. *U.S.A.* is the portrait of these two nations. It consists of *The 42nd Parallel* (1930), covering the period from 1900 up to the war; *1919* (1932), dealing with the war and the critical year of the Treaty of Versailles; and *The Big Money* (1936), which races headlong through the boom of the '20s to the bust of the '30s. Dos Passos reinforces the histories of his fictional characters with a sense of real history conveyed by the interpolated devices of "newsreels," artfully selected montages of actual newspaper headlines and popular songs of the day. He also interpolates biographies of such representative members of the establishment as the automobile maker Henry Ford, the inventor Thomas Edison, President Woodrow Wilson, and the financier J.P. Morgan. He further presents members of that "other nation" such as the Socialist Eugene V. Debs, the economist Thorstein Veblen, the labour organizer Joe Hill, and the Unknown Soldier of World War I. Yet another dimension is provided by his "camera-eye" technique: brief, poetic, personal reminiscences.

U.S.A. was followed by a less ambitious trilogy, *District of Columbia* (*Adventures of a Young Man*, 1939; *Number One*, 1943; *The Grand Design*, 1949), which chronicles Dos Passos's further disillusion with the labour movement, radical politics, and New Deal liberalism. The decline of his creative energy and the increasing political conservatism evident in these works became even more pronounced in subsequent works. At his death at 74, his books scarcely received critical attention.

THE HARLEM RENAISSANCE

The Harlem Renaissance was a blossoming (*c.* 1918–37) of African American culture, particularly in the creative arts, and the most influential movement in African American literary history. Embracing not just literary arts but musical, theatrical, and visual arts as well, participants sought to

reconceptualize "the Negro" apart from the white stereotypes that had influenced black peoples' relationship to
their heritage and to each other. They also sought to break
free of Victorian moral values and bourgeois shame about
aspects of their lives that might, as seen by whites, rein-
force racist beliefs. Never dominated by a particular school
of thought but rather characterized by intense debate, the
movement laid the groundwork for all later African
American literature and had an enormous impact on subsequent black literature and consciousness worldwide.

While the renaissance was not confined to the Harlem
district of New York City, Harlem attracted a remarkable
concentration of intellect and talent, and served as the symbolic capital of this cultural awakening. The ironies of racial
identity dominate the stories and novels produced by writers
of this period, including harsh portraits of the black middle
class in Nella Larsen's *Quicksand* (1928) and *Passing* (1929),
and the powerful stories of Langston Hughes in *The Ways
of White Folks* (1934), as well as the varied literary materials—
poetry, fiction, and drama—collected in Jean Toomer's
Cane (1923). Richard Wright's books were works of burning social protest, Dostoyevskian in their intensity, that dealt
boldly with the plight of American blacks in both the old
South and the Northern urban ghetto. Zora Neale Hurston's
training in anthropology and folklore contributed to *Their
Eyes Were Watching God* (1937), her powerful feminist novel
about the all-black Florida town in which she had grown up.

RICHARD WRIGHT

(b. Sept. 4, 1908, Roxie, Miss., U.S.—d. Nov. 28, 1960, Paris, France)

The novelist and short-story writer Richard Wright was
among the first black American writers to protest white
treatment of blacks, notably in his novel *Native Son* (1940)

and his autobiography, *Black Boy* (1945). He inaugurated the tradition of protest explored by other black writers after World War II.

Wright's grandparents had been slaves. He was born into poverty near Natchez, Miss., in 1908. His father left home when he was five, and Wright was often shifted from one relative to another. He worked at a number of jobs before joining the northward migration, first to Memphis, Tenn., and then to Chicago. There, after working in unskilled jobs, he got an opportunity to write through the Federal Writers' Project. In 1932 he became a member of the Communist Party, and in 1937 he went to New York City, where he became Harlem editor of the Communist *Daily Worker*.

He first came to the general public's attention with a volume of novellas, *Uncle Tom's Children* (1938), based on the question: How may a black man live in a country that denies his humanity? In each story but one the hero's quest ends in death.

His fictional scene shifted to Chicago in *Native Son*. Its protagonist, a poor black youth named Bigger Thomas, accidentally kills a white girl, and in the course of his ensuing flight his hitherto meaningless awareness of antagonism from a white world becomes intelligible. The book was a best-seller and was staged successfully as a play on Broadway (1941) by Orson Welles. Wright himself played Bigger Thomas in a motion-picture version made in Argentina in 1951.

In 1944 he left the Communist Party because of political and personal differences. Wright's *Black Boy* is a moving account of his childhood and young manhood in the South. The book chronicles the extreme poverty of his childhood, his experience of white prejudice and violence against blacks, and his growing awareness of his interest in literature.

After World War II, Wright settled in Paris as a permanent expatriate. *The Outsider* (1953), acclaimed as the first American existential novel, warned that the black man had awakened in a disintegrating society not ready to include him. Three later novels were not well-received. Among his polemical writings of that period was *White Man, Listen!* (1957), which was originally a series of lectures given in Europe. *Eight Men,* a collection of short stories, appeared in 1961.

The autobiographical *American Hunger,* which narrates Wright's experiences after moving to the North, was published posthumously in 1977. Some of the more candid passages dealing with race, sex, and politics in Wright's books had been cut or omitted before original publication. Unexpurgated versions of *Native Son, Black Boy,* and his other works were published in 1991, however. A novella, *Rite of Passage* (1994), and an unfinished crime novel, *A Father's Law* (2008), were also published posthumously.

ZORA NEALE HURSTON

(b. Jan. 7, 1891, Notasulga, Ala., U.S. — d. January 28, 1960, Fort Pierce, Fla.)

Zora Neale Hurston was an American folklorist and writer associated with the Harlem Renaissance who celebrated the African American culture of the rural South.

Although Hurston claimed to be born in 1901 in Eatonville, Fla., she was, in fact, 10 years older and had moved with her family to Eatonville only as a small child. There, in the first incorporated all-black town in the country, she attended school until age 13. After the death of her mother (1904), Hurston's home life became increasingly difficult, and at 16 she joined a traveling theatrical company, ending up in New York City during the Harlem Renaissance. She attended Howard University from 1921 to 1924 and in

Zora Neale Hurston. Library of Congress, Prints & Photographs Division, Carl Van Vechten Collection

1925 won a scholarship to Barnard College, where she studied anthropology under Franz Boas. She graduated from Barnard in 1928 and for two years pursued graduate studies in anthropology at Columbia University. She also conducted field studies in folklore among African Americans in the South. Her trips were funded by folklorist Charlotte Mason, who was a patron to both Hurston and Langston Hughes. For a short time Hurston was an amanuensis to novelist Fannie Hurst. In 1930 Hurston collaborated with Hughes on a play (never finished) titled *Mule Bone: A Comedy of Negro Life in Three Acts* (published posthumously 1991). In 1934 she published her first novel, *Jonah's Gourd Vine*, which was well received by critics for its portrayal of African American life uncluttered by stock figures or sentimentality. *Mules and Men*, a study of folkways among the African American population of Florida, followed in 1935. *Their Eyes Were Watching God* (1937), a novel, *Tell My Horse* (1938), a blend of travel writing and anthropology based on her investigations of voodoo in Haiti, and *Moses, Man of the Mountain* (1939), a novel, firmly established her as a major author.

For a number of years Hurston was on the faculty of North Carolina College for Negroes (now North Carolina Central University) in Durham. She also was on the staff of the Library of Congress. *Dust Tracks on a Road* (1942), an autobiography, is highly regarded. Her last book, *Seraph on the Suwanee*, a novel, appeared in 1948. Despite her early promise, by the time of her death in 1960 Hurston was little remembered by the general reading public, but there was a resurgence of interest in her work in the late 20th century. In addition to *Mule Bone*, several other collections were also published posthumously; these include *Spunk: The Selected Stories* (1985), *The Complete Stories* (1995), and *Every Tongue Got to Confess* (2001), a collection of folktales from the South. In 1995 the Library of America published a two-volume set of her work in its series.

HEMINGWAY, FAULKNER, AND STEINBECK

In the 1920s three major American authors emerged with writings that showed a shift from the disillusionment that was typical of the social critics of the era. Ernest Hemingway, William Faulkner, and John Steinbeck all believed in the power of the artist to palpably improve the broader American society, though each author strived to meet that goal in his own unique manner.

ERNEST HEMINGWAY

Ernest Hemingway's early short stories and his first novels, *The Sun Also Rises* (1926) and *A Farewell to Arms* (1929), were full of the existential disillusionment of American expatriates after World War I. The Spanish Civil War, however, led him to espouse the possibility of collective action to solve social problems. His great impact on other writers came from his deceptively simple, stripped-down prose, full of unspoken implication, and from his tough but vulnerable masculinity, which created a myth that imprisoned the author and haunted the World War II generation.

The first son of Clarence Edmonds Hemingway, a doctor, and Grace Hall Hemingway, Ernest Miller Hemingway was born in a suburb of Chicago in 1899. He was educated in the public schools and began to write in high school, where he was active and outstanding, but the parts of his boyhood that mattered most were summers spent with his family on Walloon Lake in upper Michigan. On graduation from high school in 1917, impatient for a less sheltered environment, he did not enter college but went to Kansas City, where he was employed as a reporter for the *Star*. He was repeatedly rejected for military service because of a defective eye, but he managed to enter World War I as an ambulance driver for the American Red Cross. On July 8, 1918, not yet 19 years old, he was injured on the Austro-Italian front at Fossalta di Piave. Decorated for heroism and hospitalized in Milan, he fell in love with a Red Cross nurse, Agnes von Kurowsky, who declined to marry him. These were experiences he was never to forget.

After recuperating at home, Hemingway renewed his efforts at writing, for a while worked at odd jobs in Chicago, and sailed for France as a foreign correspondent for the *Toronto Star*. Advised and encouraged by other American writers in Paris—F. Scott Fitzgerald, Gertrude Stein, Ezra Pound—he began to see his nonjournalistic work appear in print there, and in 1925 his first important book, a collection of stories called *In Our Time*, was published in New York City; it was originally released in Paris in 1924. In 1926 he published *The Sun Also Rises*, a novel with which he scored his first solid success. A pessimistic but sparkling book, it deals with a group of aimless expatriates in France and Spain—members of the postwar Lost Generation, a phrase that Hemingway scorned while making it famous. This work also introduced him to the limelight, which he both craved and resented for the rest of his life. Hemingway's *The Torrents of Spring*, a parody of the American writer Sherwood Anderson's book *Dark Laughter*, also appeared in 1926.

The writing of books occupied Hemingway for most of the postwar years. He remained based in Paris, but he traveled widely for the skiing, bullfighting, fishing, and hunting that by then had become part of his life and formed the background for much of his writing. His position as a master of short fiction had been advanced by *Men Without Women* in 1927 and thoroughly established with the stories in *Winner Take Nothing* in 1933. Among his finest stories are "The Killers," "The Short Happy Life of Francis Macomber," and "The Snows of Kilimanjaro." At least in the public view, however, the novel *A Farewell to Arms* (1929) overshadowed such works. Reaching back to his experience as a young soldier in Italy, Hemingway developed a grim but lyrical novel of great power, fusing love story with war story. While serving with the Italian ambulance service during World War I, the American lieutenant Frederic Henry falls in love with the English nurse Catherine Barkley, who tends him during his recuperation after being wounded. She becomes pregnant by him, but he must return to his post. Henry deserts during the Italians' disastrous retreat after the Battle of Caporetto, and the reunited couple flee Italy by crossing the border into Switzerland. There, however, Catherine and her baby die during childbirth, and Henry is left desolate at the loss of the great love of his life.

Hemingway's love of Spain and his passion for bullfighting resulted in *Death in the Afternoon* (1932), a learned study of a spectacle he saw more as tragic ceremony than as sport. Similarly, a safari he took in 1933–34 in the big-game region of Tanganyika resulted in *The Green Hills of Africa* (1935), an account of big-game hunting. Mostly for the fishing, he purchased a house in Key West, Fla., and bought his

Ernest Hemingway. Hulton Archive/Getty Images

own fishing boat. A minor novel of 1937 called *To Have and Have Not* is about a Caribbean desperado and is set against a background of lower-class violence and upper-class decadence in Key West during the Great Depression.

By now Spain was in the midst of civil war. Still deeply attached to that country, Hemingway made four trips there, once more a correspondent. He raised money for the Republicans in their struggle against the Nationalists under General Francisco Franco, and he wrote a play called *The Fifth Column* (1938), which is set in besieged Madrid. As in many of his books, the protagonist of the play is based on the author. Following his last visit to the Spanish war, he purchased Finca Vigía ("Lookout Farm"), an unpretentious estate outside Havana, Cuba, and went to cover another war—the Japanese invasion of China.

The harvest of Hemingway's considerable experience of Spain in war and peace was the novel *For Whom the Bell Tolls* (1940), a substantial and impressive work that some critics consider his finest novel, in preference to *A Farewell to Arms*. It was also the most successful of all his books as measured in sales. Set during the Spanish Civil War, it tells of Robert Jordan, an American volunteer who is sent to join a guerrilla band behind the Nationalist lines in the Guadarrama Mountains. Most of the novel concerns Jordan's relations with the varied personalities of the band, including the girl Maria, with whom he falls in love. Through dialogue, flashbacks, and stories, Hemingway offers telling and vivid profiles of the Spanish character and unsparingly depicts the cruelty and inhumanity stirred up by the civil war. Jordan's mission is to blow up a strategic bridge near Segovia in order to aid a coming Republican attack, which he realizes is doomed to fail. In an atmosphere of impending disaster, he blows up the bridge but is wounded and makes his retreating comrades leave him behind, where he prepares a last-minute resistance to his Nationalist pursuers.

All of his life Hemingway was fascinated by war—in *A Farewell to Arms* he focused on its pointlessness, in *For Whom the Bell Tolls* on the comradeship it creates—and, as World War II progressed, he made his way to London as a journalist. He flew several missions with the Royal Air Force and crossed the English Channel with American troops on D Day (June 6, 1944). Attaching himself to the 22nd Regiment of the 4th Infantry Division, he saw a good deal of action in Normandy and in the Battle of the Bulge. He also participated in the liberation of Paris, and, although ostensibly a journalist, he impressed professional soldiers not only as a man of courage in battle but also as a real expert in military matters, guerrilla activities, and intelligence collection.

Following the war in Europe, Hemingway returned to his home in Cuba and began to work seriously again. He also traveled widely, and, on a trip to Africa, he was injured in a plane crash. Soon after (in 1953), he received the Pulitzer Prize in fiction for *The Old Man and the Sea* (1952), a short heroic novel about an old Cuban fisherman who, after an extended struggle, hooks and boats a giant marlin only to have it eaten by voracious sharks during the long voyage home. This book, which played a role in gaining for Hemingway the Nobel Prize for Literature in 1954, was as enthusiastically praised as his previous novel, *Across the River and into the Trees* (1950), the story of a professional army officer who dies while on leave in Venice, had been damned.

By 1960 Fidel Castro's revolution had driven Hemingway from Cuba. He settled in Ketchum, Idaho, and tried to lead his life and do his work as before. For a while he succeeded, but, anxiety-ridden and depressed, he was twice hospitalized at the Mayo Clinic in Rochester, Minn., where he received electroshock treatments. Two days after his return to the house in Ketchum in the summer of 1961, he took his life with a shotgun. Hemingway had married four times and fathered three sons.

Hemingway left behind a substantial amount of manuscript, some of which has been published. *A Moveable Feast*, an entertaining memoir of his years in Paris (1921–26) before he was famous, was issued in 1964. *Islands in the Stream*, three closely related novellas growing directly out of his peacetime memories of the Caribbean island of Bimini, of Havana during World War II, and of searching for U-boats off Cuba, appeared in 1970.

Hemingway's characters plainly embody his own values and view of life. The main characters of *The Sun Also Rises*, *A Farewell to Arms*, and *For Whom the Bell Tolls* are young men whose strength and self-confidence nevertheless coexist with a sensitivity that leaves them deeply scarred by their wartime experiences. War was for Hemingway a potent symbol of the world, which he viewed as complex, filled with moral ambiguities, and offering almost unavoidable pain, hurt, and destruction. To survive in such a world, and perhaps emerge victorious, one must conduct oneself with honour, courage, endurance, and dignity, a set of principles known as "the Hemingway code." To behave well in the lonely, losing battle with life is to show "grace under pressure" and constitutes in itself a

Lost Generation

In general the Lost Generation was the post–World War I generation, but specifically it was a group of U.S. writers who came of age during the war and established their literary reputations in the 1920s. The term stems from a remark made by Gertrude Stein to Ernest Hemingway, "You are all a lost generation." Hemingway used it as an epigraph to *The Sun Also Rises* (1926), a novel that captures the attitudes of a hard-drinking, fast-living set of disillusioned young expatriates in postwar Paris.

The generation was "lost" in the sense that its inherited values were no longer relevant in the postwar world and because of its spiritual alienation from a U.S. that, basking under Pres. Warren G. Harding's "back to normalcy" policy, seemed to its members to be hopelessly provincial, materialistic, and emotionally barren. The term embraces Hemingway, F. Scott Fitzgerald, John Dos Passos, E.E. Cummings, Archibald MacLeish, Hart Crane, and many other writers who made Paris the centre of their literary activities in the '20s. They were never a literary school. In the 1930s, as these writers turned in different directions, their works lost the distinctive stamp of the postwar period. The last representative works of the era were Fitzgerald's *Tender Is the Night* (1934) and Dos Passos's *The Big Money* (1936).

kind of victory, a theme clearly established in *The Old Man and the Sea*.

Hemingway's prose style was probably the most widely imitated of any in the 20th century. He wished to strip his own use of language of inessentials, ridding it of all traces of verbosity, embellishment, and sentimentality. In striving to be as objective and honest as possible, Hemingway hit upon the device of describing a series of actions by using short, simple sentences from which all comment or emotional rhetoric has been eliminated. These sentences are composed largely of nouns and verbs, have few adjectives and adverbs, and rely on repetition and rhythm for much of their effect. The resulting terse, concentrated prose is concrete and unemotional yet is often resonant and capable of conveying great irony through understatement. Hemingway's use of dialogue was similarly fresh, simple, and natural-sounding. The influence of this style was felt worldwide wherever novels were written, particularly from the 1930s through the '50s.

A consummately contradictory man, Hemingway achieved a fame surpassed by few, if any, American authors of the 20th century. The virile nature of his writing, which attempted to re-create the exact physical sensations he experienced in wartime, big-game hunting, and bullfighting, in fact masked an aesthetic sensibility of great delicacy. He was a celebrity long before he reached middle age, but his popularity continues to be validated by serious critical opinion.

WILLIAM FAULKNER

Hemingway's great rival as a stylist and mythmaker was William Faulkner, whose writing was as baroque as Hemingway's was spare. Influenced by Sherwood Anderson, Herman Melville, and especially James Joyce, Faulkner combined stream-of-consciousness techniques with rich social history. Works such as *The Sound and the Fury* (1929), *As I Lay Dying* (1930), *Light in August* (1932), and *The Hamlet* (1940) were parts of the unfolding history of Yoknapatawpha County, a mythical Mississippi community, which depicted the transformation and the decadence of the South. Faulkner's work was dominated by a sense of guilt going back to the American Civil War and the appropriation of Indian lands. Though often comic, his work pictured the disintegration of the leading families and showed a growing concern with the troubled role of race in Southern life.

YOUTH AND EARLY WRITINGS

As the eldest of the four sons of Murry Cuthbert and Maud Butler Falkner, William Faulkner (as he later spelled his name) was well aware of his family background and especially of his great-grandfather, Colonel William Clark Falkner, a colourful if violent figure who fought gallantly during the Civil War, built a local railway, and published a popular romantic novel called *The White Rose of Memphis*. Born in 1897 in New Albany, Miss., Faulkner soon moved with his parents to nearby Ripley and then to the town of Oxford, the seat of Lafayette county, where his father later became business manager of the University of Mississippi. In Oxford he experienced the characteristic open-air upbringing of a Southern white youth of middle-class parents: he had a pony to ride and was introduced to guns and hunting. A reluctant student, he left high school without graduating but devoted himself to "undirected reading," first in isolation and later under the guidance of Phil Stone, a family friend who combined study and practice of the law with lively literary interests and was a constant source of current books and magazines.

In July 1918, impelled by dreams of martial glory and by despair at a broken love affair, Faulkner joined the British Royal Air Force (RAF) as a cadet pilot under training in Canada, although the November 1918 armistice intervened before he could finish ground school, let alone fly or reach Europe. After returning home, he enrolled for a few university courses, published poems and drawings in campus newspapers, and acted out a self-dramatizing role as a poet who had seen wartime service. After working in a New York bookstore for three months in the fall of 1921, he returned to Oxford and ran the university post office there with notorious laxness until forced to resign. In 1924 Phil Stone's financial assistance enabled him to publish *The Marble Faun,* a pastoral verse-sequence in rhymed octosyllabic couplets. There were also early short stories, but Faulkner's first sustained attempt to write fiction occurred during a six-month visit to New Orleans—then a significant literary centre—that began in January 1925 and ended in early July with his departure for a five-month tour of Europe, including several weeks in Paris.

His first novel, *Soldiers' Pay* (1926), given a Southern though not a Mississippian setting, was an impressive achievement, stylistically ambitious and strongly evocative of the sense of alienation experienced by soldiers returning from World War I to a civilian world of which they seemed no longer a part. A second novel, *Mosquitoes* (1927), launched a satirical attack on the New Orleans literary scene, including identifiable individuals, and can perhaps best be read as a declaration of artistic independence. Back in Oxford—with occasional visits to Pascagoula on the Gulf Coast—Faulkner again worked at a series of temporary jobs but was chiefly concerned with proving himself as a professional writer. None of his short stories was accepted, however, and he was especially shaken by his difficulty in finding a publisher for *Flags in the Dust* (published posthumously, 1973), a long, leisurely novel, drawing extensively on local observation and his own family history, that he had confidently counted upon to establish his reputation and career. When the novel eventually did appear, severely truncated, as *Sartoris* in 1929, it created in print for the first time that densely imagined world of Jefferson and Yoknapatawpha County—based partly on Ripley but chiefly on Oxford and Lafayette county and characterized by frequent recurrences of the same characters, places, and themes—which Faulkner was to use as the setting for so many subsequent novels and stories.

THE MAJOR NOVELS

Faulkner had meanwhile "written [his] guts" into the more technically sophisticated *The Sound and the Fury,* believing that he was fated to remain permanently unpublished and need therefore make no concessions to the cautious commercialism of the literary marketplace. The novel did find a publisher, despite the difficulties it posed for its readers, and from the moment of its appearance in October 1929 Faulkner drove confidently forward as a writer, engaging always with new themes, new areas of experience, and, above all, new technical challenges. Crucial to his extraordinary early productivity was the decision to shun the talk, infighting, and publicity of literary centres and live instead in what was then the small-town remoteness of Oxford, where he was already at home and could devote himself, in near isolation, to actual writing. In 1929 he married Estelle Oldham—whose previous marriage, now terminated, had helped drive him into the RAF in 1918. One year later he bought Rowan Oak, a handsome but run-down pre–Civil War house on the outskirts of Oxford, restoration work on the house becoming, along with hunting, an important diversion in the years ahead. A daughter, Jill, was born to the couple in 1933, and although their marriage was otherwise troubled, Faulkner remained working at home throughout the 1930s and '40s, except when financial need forced him to accept the Hollywood screenwriting assignments he deplored but very competently fulfilled.

Oxford provided Faulkner with intimate access to a deeply conservative rural world, conscious of its past and remote from the urban-industrial mainstream, in terms of which he could work out the moral as well as narrative patterns of his work. His fictional methods, however, were the reverse of conservative. He knew the work not only of Honoré de Balzac, Gustave Flaubert, Charles Dickens, and Herman Melville but also of Joseph Conrad, James Joyce, Sherwood Anderson, and other recent figures on both sides of the Atlantic, and in *The Sound and the Fury* (1929), his first major novel, he combined a Yoknapatawpha setting with radical technical experimentation. In successive "stream-of-consciousness" monologues the three brothers of Candace (Caddy) Compson—Benjy the idiot, Quentin the disturbed Harvard undergraduate, and Jason the embittered local businessman—expose their differing obsessions with their sister and their loveless relationships with their parents. A fourth section, narrated as if authorially, provides new perspectives on some of the central characters, including Dilsey, the Compsons' black servant, and moves toward a powerful yet essentially unresolved conclusion.

William Faulkner. Hulton Archive/ Getty Images

Faulkner's next novel, the brilliant tragicomedy called *As I Lay Dying* (1930), is centred upon the conflicts within the "poor white" Bundren family as it makes its slow and difficult way to Jefferson to bury its matriarch's malodorously decaying corpse. Entirely narrated by the various Bundrens and people encountered on their journey, it is the most systematically multivoiced of Faulkner's novels and marks the culmination of his early post-Joycean experimentalism.

Although the psychological intensity and technical innovation of these two novels were scarcely calculated to ensure a large contemporary readership, Faulkner's name was beginning to be known in the early 1930s, and he was able to place short stories even in such popular—and well-paying—magazines as *Collier's* and *Saturday Evening Post*. Greater, if more equivocal, prominence came with the financially successful publication of *Sanctuary*, a novel about the brutal rape of a Southern college student and its generally violent, sometimes comic, consequences. A serious work, despite Faulkner's unfortunate declaration that it was written merely to make money, *Sanctuary* was actually completed prior to *As I Lay Dying* and published, in February 1931, only after Faulkner had gone to the trouble and expense of restructuring and partly rewriting it—though without moderating the violence—at proof stage.

Despite the demands of film work and short stories (of which a first collection appeared in 1931 and a second in 1934), and even the preparation of a volume of poems (published in 1933 as *A Green Bough*), Faulkner produced in 1932 another long and powerful novel. Complexly structured and involving several major characters, *Light in August* revolves primarily upon the contrasted careers of Lena Grove, a pregnant young countrywoman serenely in pursuit of her biological destiny, and Joe Christmas, a dark-complexioned orphan uncertain as to his racial origins, whose life becomes a desperate and often violent search for a sense of personal identity, a secure location on one side or the other of the tragic dividing line of colour.

Made temporarily affluent by *Sanctuary* and Hollywood, Faulkner took up flying in the early 1930s, bought a Waco cabin aircraft, and flew it in February 1934 to the dedication of Shushan Airport in New Orleans, gathering there much of the material for *Pylon*, the novel about racing and barnstorming pilots that he published in 1935. Having given the Waco to his youngest brother, Dean, and encouraged him to become a professional pilot, Faulkner was both grief- and guilt-stricken when Dean crashed and died in the plane later in 1935. When Dean's daughter was born in 1936, he took responsibility for her education.

The experience perhaps contributed to the emotional intensity of the novel on which he was then working. In *Absalom, Absalom!* (1936) Thomas Sutpen arrives in Jefferson from "nowhere," ruthlessly carves a large plantation out of the Mississippi wilderness, fights valiantly in the Civil War in defense of his adopted society, but is ultimately destroyed by his inhumanity toward those whom he has used and cast aside in the obsessive pursuit of his grandiose dynastic "design." By refusing to acknowledge his first, partly black son, Charles Bon, Sutpen also loses his second son, Henry, who goes into hiding after killing Bon (whom he loves) in the name of their sister's honour. Because this profoundly Southern story is constructed—speculatively, conflictingly, and inconclusively—by a series of narrators with sharply divergent self-interested perspectives, *Absalom, Absalom!* is often seen, in its infinite open-endedness, as Faulkner's supreme "modernist" fiction, focused above all on the processes of its own telling.

LATER LIFE AND WORKS

The novel *The Wild Palms* (1939) was again technically adventurous, with two distinct yet thematically counterpointed narratives alternating, chapter by chapter, throughout. But Faulkner was beginning to return to the Yoknapatawpha County material he had first imagined in the 1920s and subsequently exploited in short-story form. *The Unvanquished* (1938) was relatively conventional, but *The Hamlet* (1940), the first volume of the long-uncompleted "Snopes" trilogy, emerged as a work of extraordinary stylistic richness. Its episodic structure is underpinned by recurrent thematic patterns and by the wryly humorous presence of V.K. Ratliff—an itinerant sewing-machine agent—and his unavailing opposition to the increasing power and prosperity of the supremely manipulative Flem Snopes and his numerous "poor white" relatives. In 1942 appeared *Go Down, Moses,* yet another major work, in which an intense exploration of the linked themes of racial, sexual, and environmental exploitation is conducted largely in terms of the complex interactions between the "white" and "black" branches of the plantation-owning McCaslin family, especially as represented by Isaac McCaslin on the one hand and Lucas Beauchamp on the other.

For various reasons—the constraints on wartime publishing, financial pressures to take on more scriptwriting, difficulties with the work later published as *A Fable*—Faulkner did not produce another novel until *Intruder in the Dust* (1948), in which Lucas Beauchamp, reappearing from *Go Down, Moses,* is proved innocent of murder, and thus saved from lynching, only by the persistent efforts of a young white boy. Racial issues were again confronted, but in the somewhat ambiguous terms that were to mark Faulkner's later public statements on race: while deeply sympathetic to the oppression suffered by blacks in the Southern states, he nevertheless felt that such wrongs should be righted by the South itself, free of Northern intervention.

Faulkner's American reputation—which had always lagged well behind his reputation in Europe—was boosted by *The Portable Faulkner* (1946), an anthology skillfully edited by Malcolm Cowley in accordance with the arresting if questionable thesis that Faulkner was deliberately constructing a historically based "legend" of the South. Faulkner's *Collected Stories* (1950), impressive in both quantity and quality, was also well received, and later in 1950

Malcolm Cowley

(b. Aug. 24, 1898, Belsano, Pa., U.S. — d. March 27, 1989, New Milford, Conn.)

An American literary critic and social historian, Malcolm Cowley chronicled the writers of the "Lost Generation" of the 1920s and their successors. As literary editor of *The New Republic* from 1929 to 1944, with a generally leftist position on cultural questions, he played a significant part in many of the literary and political battles of the Great Depression years.

Cowley grew up in Pittsburgh. His education at Harvard was interrupted during World War I when he joined the American Field Service as an ambulance driver in France and attended for a brief period a U.S. Army artillery officers' training school. He graduated cum laude from Harvard in 1920, took advanced study in France at the University of Montpellier (1922), and helped to put out the expatriate little magazines *Secession* and *Broom*. In this role, he came to know the European and particularly the Parisian avant-garde. (The two magazines were quartered in various European cities, and each had for a time as associate editor the American biographer Matthew Josephson.) Cowley returned to the United States in 1923 and for the next five years supported himself by freelance writing and translating; he eventually settled in Sherman, Conn. His *Exile's Return: A Narrative of Ideas* (1934; rev. ed. published 1951 under the subtitle *A Literary Odyssey of the 1920's*) is an important social and literary history of the expatriate American writers of the 1920s. In it he signaled the importance of their rediscovery of America as a source for literature. Cowley revived the literary reputation of William Faulkner with his editing of the anthology *The Portable Faulkner* (1946).

Among Cowley's other works are *The Literary Situation* (1954), a study of the role of the American writer in his society, and the collections of criticism and comment *Think Back on Us* (1967) and *A Many-Windowed House* (1970). The correspondence he exchanged with Faulkner appeared in 1966 in *The*

Faulkner-Cowley File: Letters and Memories, 1944–1962. Among the many books he edited are *After the Genteel Tradition: American Writers Since 1910* (1937, reprinted 1964) and *Books That Changed Our Minds* (1939). *And I Worked at the Writer's Trade* (1978) combines literary history and autobiography. In 1980 he published the well-received *The Dream of the Golden Mountains: Remembering the 1930s,* a social and cultural history of the Great Depression and the New Deal. In that year, too, he released *The View from 80,* an absorbing, honest essay on old age, expanded from an earlier magazine article.

the award of the Nobel Prize for Literature catapulted the author instantly to the peak of world fame and enabled him to affirm, in a famous acceptance speech, his belief in the survival of the human race, even in an atomic age, and in the importance of the artist to that survival.

The Nobel Prize had a major impact on Faulkner's private life. Confident now of his reputation and future sales, he became less consistently "driven" as a writer than in earlier years and allowed himself more personal freedom, drinking heavily at times and indulging in a number of extramarital affairs—his opportunities in these directions being considerably enhanced by a final screenwriting assignment in Egypt in 1954 and several overseas trips (most notably to Japan in 1955) undertaken on behalf of the U.S. State Department. He took his "ambassadorial" duties seriously, speaking frequently in public and to interviewers, and also became politically active at home, taking positions on major racial issues in the vain hope of finding middle ground between entrenched Southern conservatives and interventionist Northern liberals. Local Oxford opinion proving hostile to such views, Faulkner in 1957 and 1958 readily accepted semester-long appointments as writer-in-residence at the University of Virginia in Charlottesville. Attracted to the town by the presence of his daughter and her children as well as by its opportunities for horse-riding and fox-hunting, Faulkner bought a house there in 1959, though continuing to spend time at Rowan Oak.

The quality of Faulkner's writing is often said to have declined in the wake of the Nobel Prize. But the central sections of *Requiem for a Nun* (1951) are challengingly set out in dramatic form, and *A Fable* (1954), a long, densely written, and complexly structured novel about World War I, demands attention as the work in which Faulkner made by far his greatest investment of time, effort, and authorial commitment. In *The Town* (1957) and *The Mansion* (1959) Faulkner not only brought the "Snopes" trilogy to its conclusion, carrying his Yoknapatawpha narrative to beyond the end of World War II, but subtly varied the management of narrative point of view. Finally, in June 1962 Faulkner published yet another distinctive novel, the genial, nostalgic comedy of male maturation he called *The Reivers* and appropriately subtitled "A Reminiscence." A month later he was dead, of a heart attack, at the age of 64, his health undermined by his drinking and by too many falls from horses too big for him.

ASSESSMENT

By the time of his death Faulkner had clearly emerged not just as the major American novelist of his generation but as one of the greatest writers of the 20th century, unmatched for his extraordinary structural and stylistic resourcefulness, for the range and depth of his characterization and social notation, and for his persistence and success in exploring fundamental human issues in intensely localized terms. Some critics, early and late, have found his work extravagantly rhetorical and unduly violent, and there have been strong objections, especially late in the

20th century, to the perceived insensitivity of his portrayals of women and black Americans. His reputation, grounded in the sheer scale and scope of his achievement, seems nonetheless secure, and he remains a profoundly influential presence for novelists writing in the United States, South America, and, indeed, throughout the world.

JOHN STEINBECK

The American novelist John Steinbeck is best known for *The Grapes of Wrath* (1939), which summed up the bitterness of the Great Depression decade and aroused widespread sympathy for the plight of migratory farm workers. He also showed his affinity for colourful outcasts, such as the *paisanos* of the Monterey area, in the short novels *Tortilla Flat* (1935), *Of Mice and Men* (1937), and *Cannery Row* (1945).

Steinbeck was born in Salinas, Calif., in 1902, and he attended Stanford University, Stanford, Calif., intermittently between 1920 and 1926 but did not take a degree. Before his books attained success, he spent considerable time supporting himself as a manual labourer while writing, and his experiences lent authenticity to his depictions of the lives of the workers in his stories. He spent much of his life in Monterey county, Calif., which later was the setting of some of his fiction.

Steinbeck's first novel, *Cup of Gold* (1929), in which he voiced a distrust of society and glorified the anarchistic individualist typical of the rebellious 1920s, was followed by *The Pastures of Heaven* (1932) and *To a God Unknown* (1933), none of which were successful. He first achieved popularity with *Tortilla Flat* (1935), an affectionately told story of Mexican-Americans. The mood of gentle humour turned to one of unrelenting grimness in his next novel, *In*

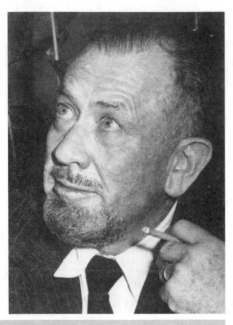

John Steinbeck. Keystone/Hulton Archive/Getty Images

Dubious Battle (1936), a classic account of a strike by agricultural labourers and a pair of Marxist labour organizers who engineer it. The novella *Of Mice and Men* (1937), which also appeared in play and film versions, is a tragic story about the strange, complex bond between two migrant labourers. *The Grapes of Wrath* won a Pulitzer Prize and a National Book Award and was made into a notable film in 1940. A protest novel punctuated by prose-poem interludes, *The Grapes of Wrath* tells the story of the migration of the Joads, an Oklahoma Dust Bowl family, to California. During their almost biblical journey, they learn the necessity for collective action among the poor and downtrodden to prevent them from being destroyed individually.

After the best-selling success of *The Grapes of Wrath,* Steinbeck went to Mexico to collect marine life with the freelance biologist Edward F. Ricketts, and the two men collaborated in writing *Sea of Cortez* (1941), a study of the fauna of the Gulf of California. During World War II Steinbeck wrote some effective pieces of government propaganda, among them *The Moon Is Down* (1942), a novel of Norwegians under the Nazis, and he also served as a war correspondent. His immediate postwar work—*Cannery Row* (1945), *The Pearl* (1947), and *The Wayward Bus* (1947)—contained the familiar elements of his social criticism but were more relaxed in approach and sentimental in tone.

Steinbeck's later writings were comparatively slight works of entertainment and journalism interspersed with three conscientious attempts to reassert his stature as a major novelist: *Burning Bright* (1950), *East of Eden* (1952), and *The Winter of Our Discontent* (1961). In critical opinion, none equaled his earlier achievement. *East of Eden,* an ambitious epic about the moral relations between a California farmer and his two sons, was made into a film in 1955. Steinbeck himself wrote the scripts for the film versions of his stories *The Pearl* (1948) and *The Red Pony* (1949). Outstanding among the scripts he wrote directly for motion pictures were *Forgotten Village* (1941) and *Viva Zapata!* (1952). Steinbeck died in New York City in 1968.

Steinbeck's reputation rests mostly on the naturalistic novels with proletarian themes he wrote in the 1930s; it is in these works that his building of rich symbolic structures and his attempts at conveying mythopoeic and archetypal qualities in his characters are most effective.

LYRIC FICTIONISTS

An interesting development in fiction, abetted by modernism, was a shift from naturalistic to poetic writing. There was an increased tendency to select details and endow them with symbolic meaning, set down the thought processes and emotions of the characters, and make use of rhythmic prose. In varied ways Stephen Crane, Frank Norris, Cabell, Dos Passos, Hemingway, Steinbeck, and Faulkner all showed evidence of this—in passages, in short stories, and even in entire novels. Faulkner showed the tendency at its worst in *A Fable* (1954), which, ironically, won a Pulitzer Prize.

Lyricism was especially prominent in the writings of Willa Cather. *O Pioneers!* (1913), *The Song of the Lark* (1915), and *My Ántonia* (1918) contained poetic passages about the disappearing frontier and the creative efforts of frontier folk. *A Lost Lady* (1923) and *The Professor's House* (1925) were elegiac and spare in style, though they also depicted historic social transformations, and *Death Comes for the Archbishop* (1927) was an exaltation of the past and of spiritual pioneering. Katherine Anne Porter, whose works took the form primarily of novelettes and stories, wrote more in the style of the Metaphysical poets, though she also wrote one long, ambitious novel, *Ship of Fools* (1962). Her use of the stream-of-consciousness method in *Flowering Judas* (1930) as well as in *Pale Horse, Pale Rider* (1939) had the complexity, the irony, and the symbolic sophistication characteristic of these poets, whose work the Modernists had brought into fashion.

Two of the most intensely lyrical works of the 1930s were autobiographical novels set in the Jewish ghetto of New York City's Lower East Side before World War I: Michael Gold's harsh *Jews Without Money* (1930) and Henry Roth's Proustian *Call It Sleep* (1934). They followed in the footsteps of Anzia Yezierska, a prolific writer of the 1920s whose passionate books about immigrant Jews, especially *Bread Givers* (1925), have been rediscovered by contemporary feminists.

Another lyrical and autobiographical writer was Thomas Wolfe, who put all his strivings, thoughts, and feelings into works such as *Look Homeward, Angel* (1929) and *Of Time and the River* (1935) before his early death in 1938. These Whitmanesque books, as well as posthumously edited ones such as *The Web and the Rock* (1939) and *You Can't Go Home Again* (1940), dealt with a figure much like Wolfe, echoing the author's youth in the South, young manhood in the North, and eternal search to fulfill a vision. Though grandiose, they influenced many young writers, including Jack Kerouac.

WILLA CATHER

(b. Dec. 7, 1873, near Winchester, Va., U.S.—d. April 24, 1947, New York, N.Y.)

The American novelist Willa Cather is noted for her portrayals of the settlers and frontier life on the American plains.

At age nine Cather moved with her family from Virginia to frontier Nebraska, where from age 10 she lived in the village of Red Cloud. There she grew up among the immigrants from Europe—Swedes, Bohemians, Russians, and Germans—who were breaking the land on the Great Plains.

At the University of Nebraska she showed a marked talent for journalism and story writing, and on graduating in 1895 she obtained a position in Pittsburgh, Pa., on a family magazine. Later she worked as copy editor and music and drama editor of the *Pittsburgh Leader.* She turned to teaching in 1901 and in 1903 published her first book of verses, *April Twilights.* In 1905, after the publication of her first collection of short stories, *The Troll Garden,* she was appointed managing editor of *McClure's,* the New York muckraking monthly. After building up its declining circulation, she left in 1912 to devote herself wholly to writing novels.

Cather's first novel, *Alexander's Bridge* (1912), was a factitious story of cosmopolitan life. Under the influence of Sarah Orne Jewett's regionalism, however, she turned to her familiar Nebraska material. With *O Pioneers!* (1913) and *My Ántonia* (1918), which has frequently been adjudged her finest achievement, she found her characteristic themes—the spirit and courage of the frontier she had known in her youth. *One of Ours* (1922), which won the Pulitzer Prize, and *A Lost Lady* (1923) mourned the passing of the pioneer spirit.

Willa Cather. Encyclopædia Britannica, Inc.

In her earlier *Song of the Lark* (1915), as well as in the tales assembled in *Youth and the Bright Medusa* (1920), including the much-anthologized "Paul's Case," and *Lucy Gayheart* (1935), Cather reflected the other side of her experience—the struggle of a talent to emerge from the constricting life of the prairies and the stifling effects of small-town life.

A mature statement of both themes can be found in *Obscure Destinies* (1932). With success and middle age, however, Cather experienced a strong disillusionment, which was reflected in *The Professor's House* (1925) and her essays *Not Under Forty* (1936).

Her solution was to write of the pioneer spirit of another age, that of the French Catholic missionaries in the Southwest in *Death Comes for the Archbishop* (1927) and of the French Canadians at Quebec in *Shadows on the Rock* (1931). For the setting of her last novel, *Sapphira and the Slave Girl* (1940), she used the Virginia of her ancestors and her childhood.

KATHERINE ANNE PORTER

(b. May 15, 1890, Indian Creek, Texas, U.S.—d. Sept. 18, 1980, Silver Spring, Md.)

Katherine Anne Porter was an American novelist and short-story writer, a master stylist whose long short stories have a richness of texture and complexity of character delineation usually achieved only in the novel.

Porter was educated at private and convent schools in the South. She worked as a newspaperwoman in Chicago and in Denver, Colo., before leaving in 1920 for Mexico, the scene of several of her stories. "Maria Concepcion," her first published story (1922), was included in her first book of stories, *Flowering Judas* (1930), which was enlarged in 1935 with other stories.

The title story of her next collection, *Pale Horse, Pale Rider* (1939), is a poignant tale of youthful romance brutally thwarted by the young man's death in the influenza epidemic of 1919. In it and the two other stories of the volume, "Noon Wine" and "Old Mortality," appears for the first time her semiautobiographical heroine, Miranda, a spirited and independent woman.

Porter's reputation was firmly established, but none of her books sold widely, and she supported herself primarily through fellowships, by working occasionally as an uncredited screenwriter in Hollywood, and by serving as writer-in-residence at a succession of colleges and universities. She published *The Leaning Tower* (1944), a collection of stories, and won an O. Henry Award for her 1962 story, "Holiday." The literary world awaited with great anticipation the appearance of Porter's only full-length novel, on which she had been working since 1941.

With the publication of *Ship of Fools* in 1962, Porter won a large readership for the first time. A best-seller that became a major film in 1965, it tells of the ocean voyage of a group of Germans back to their homeland from Mexico in 1931, on the eve of Hitler's ascendency. Porter's carefully crafted, ironic style is perfectly suited to the allegorical exploration of the collusion of good and evil that is her theme, and the penetrating psychological insight that had always marked her work is evident in the book.

Porter's *Collected Short Stories* (1965) won the National Book Award and the Pulitzer Prize for fiction. Her essays, articles, and book reviews were collected in *The Days Before* (1952; augmented 1970). Her last work, published in 1977, when she suffered a disabling stroke, was *The Never-Ending Wrong*, dealing with the Sacco-Vanzetti case of the 1920s.

HENRY ROTH

(b. Feb. 8, 1906, Tysmenica, Galicia, Austria-Hungary [now in Ukraine]—d. Oct. 13, 1995, Albuquerque, N.M., U.S.)

Henry Roth was an American teacher, farmer, machinist, and sporadic author whose novel *Call It Sleep* (1934) was one of the neglected masterpieces of American literature in the 1930s.

The son of Jewish immigrants, Roth graduated from the College of the City of New York in 1928 and held a variety of jobs thereafter. His novel *Call It Sleep* appeared in 1934 to laudatory reviews and sold 4,000 copies before it went out of print and was apparently forgotten. But in the late 1950s and '60s, Alfred Kazin, Irving Howe, and other American literary figures were able to revive public interest in the book, which came to be recognized as a classic of Jewish-American literature and as an important proletarian novel of the 1930s. Roth himself published virtually nothing for 30 years after the book's appearance and contented himself with tutoring, raising waterfowl on a farm, and rearing a family. He began writing again in the late 1960s, and his second book, *Shifting Landscape: A Composite, 1925–87,* a collection of short stories and essays, appeared in 1987. His novel *Mercy of a Rude Stream: A Star Shines Over Mt. Morris Park* (1994) was the first of a projected six-volume work that returned to the themes of *Call*

It Sleep. A second volume, *A Diving Rock on the Hudson,* was published in 1995.

Call It Sleep centres on the character and perceptions of a young boy who is the son of Yiddish-speaking Jewish immigrants living in a ghetto in New York City. Roth uses stream-of-consciousness techniques to show the boy's psychological development and to relay his perceptions of his family and of the larger world around him. The book powerfully evokes the terrors and anxieties the child experiences in his anguished relations with his father, and the squalid urban environment in which the family lives is realistically described.

CHAPTER 4

DRAMA AND POETRY FROM 1914 TO 1945

The groundbreaking modernism that was found in the fiction of wartime America also made an impact on the drama and poetry of the era. The country's drama was utterly transformed from a medium primarily dedicated to entertainment to something of serious literary merit. Meanwhile, American poetry, which had already begun its own major stylistic revolution in the work of Walt Whitman, further digressed from the relatively staid poetry of the 19th century.

EXPERIMENTS IN DRAMA

Although drama had not been a major art form in the 19th century, no type of writing was more experimental than a new drama that arose in rebellion against the glib commercial stage. In the early years of the 20th century, Americans traveling in Europe encountered a vital, flourishing theatre. Returning home, some of them became active in revitalizing theatre throughout the country. The Little Theatre movement in the U.S. sought to free dramatic forms and methods of production from the limitations of the large commercial theatres by establishing small experimental centres of drama.

Freed from commercial limitations, playwrights experimented with dramatic forms and methods of production, and in time producers, actors, and dramatists appeared

Little Theatre Movement

The Little Theatre movement was initiated at the beginning of the 20th century by young dramatists, stage designers, and actors who were influenced by the vital European theatre of the late 19th century; they were especially impressed by the revolutionary theories of the German director Max Reinhardt, the designing concepts of Adolphe Appia and Gordon Craig, and the staging experiments at such theatres as the Théâtre-Libre of Paris, the Freie Bühne in Berlin, and the Moscow Art Theatre. Community playhouses such as the Toy Theatre in Boston (1912), the Little Theatre in Chicago (1912), and the Little Theatre, New York City (1912) were centres of the experimental activity.

Some groups owned or leased their own theatres; a few, such as the Washington Square Players (1915), the predecessor of the Theatre Guild (1918), became important commercial producers. By encouraging freedom of expression, staging the works of talented young writers, and choosing plays solely on the basis of artistic merit, the little theatres provided a valuable early opportunity for such playwrights as Eugene O'Neill, George S. Kaufman, Elmer Rice, Maxwell Anderson, and Robert E. Sherwood.

Comparable theatres were also established in Canada around the same time. The Arts and Letters Club (1908), the Hart House Theatre at the University of Toronto (1919), and the Play Workshop (1934) are all notable examples. As in the United States, many of the playwrights who got their start in these theatres including Herman Voaden, Merrill Denison, and W.A. Tremayne—went on to anchor early professional theatres.

who had been trained in college classrooms and community playhouses. Some Little Theatre groups became commercial producers—for example, the Washington Square Players, founded in 1915, which became the Theatre Guild (first production in 1919). The resulting drama was marked by a spirit of innovation and by a new seriousness and maturity.

EUGENE O'NEILL

Eugene O'Neill, the most admired dramatist of the period, was a product of this movement. He worked with the Provincetown Players before his plays were commercially produced. His dramas were remarkable for their range. *Beyond the Horizon* (first performed 1920), *Anna Christie* (1921), *Desire Under the Elms* (1924), *The Iceman Cometh* (1946), and his masterpiece, *Long Day's Journey into Night* (produced posthumously 1956), were naturalistic works, while *The Emperor Jones* (1920) and *The Hairy Ape* (1922) made use of the Expressionistic techniques developed in German drama in the period 1914–24. He also employed a stream-of-consciousness form of psychological mono-logue in *Strange Interlude* (1928) and produced a work that combined myth, family drama, and psychological analysis in *Mourning Becomes Electra* (1931).

EARLY LIFE

O'Neill was born into the theatre. His father, James O'Neill, was a successful touring actor in the last quarter of the 19th century whose most famous role was that of the Count of Monte Cristo in a stage adaptation of the Alexandre Dumas *père* novel. His mother, Ella, accompanied her hus-band back and forth across the country, settling down only briefly for the birth of her first son, James, Jr., and of Eugene.

Eugene, who was born in a hotel in 1888, spent his early childhood in hotel rooms, on trains, and backstage. Although he later deplored the nightmare insecurity of his early years and blamed his father for the difficult, rough-and-tumble life the family led—a life that resulted in his mother's drug addiction—Eugene had the theatre in his blood. He was also, as a child, steeped in the peasant

Irish Catholicism of his father and the more genteel, mystical piety of his mother, two influences, often in dramatic conflict, which account for the high sense of drama and the struggle with God and religion that distinguish O'Neill's plays.

O'Neill was educated at boarding schools—Mt. St. Vincent in the Bronx and Betts Academy in Stamford, Conn. His summers were spent at the family's only permanent home, a modest house overlooking the Thames River in New London, Conn. He attended Princeton University for one year (1906–07), after which he left school to begin what he later regarded as his real education in "life experience." The next six years very nearly ended his life. He shipped to sea, lived a derelict's existence on the waterfronts of Buenos Aires, Liverpool, and New York City, submerged himself in alcohol, and attempted suicide. Recovering briefly at the age of 24, he held a job for a few months as a reporter and contributor to the poetry column of the *New London Telegraph* but soon came down with tuberculosis. Confined to the Gaylord Farm Sanitarium in Wallingford, Conn., for six months (1912–13), he confronted himself soberly and nakedly for the first time and seized the chance for what he later called his "rebirth." He began to write plays.

ENTRY INTO THEATRE

O'Neill's first efforts were awkward melodramas, but they were about people and subjects—prostitutes, derelicts, lonely sailors, God's injustice to man—that had, up to that time, been in the province of serious novels and were not considered fit subjects for presentation on the American stage. A theatre critic persuaded his father to send him to Harvard to study with George Pierce Baker in his famous playwriting course. Although what O'Neill produced

Eugene O'Neill with his family. The son of an actor, O'Neill achieved his own theatrical success as a noted playwright. His dramas are considered classics of the stage. Hulton Archive/Getty Images

during that year (1914–15) owed little to Baker's academic instruction, the chance to work steadily at writing set him firmly on his chosen path.

O'Neill's first appearance as a playwright came in the summer of 1916, in the quiet fishing village of Provincetown, Mass., where a group of young writers and painters had launched an experimental theatre. In their tiny, ramshackle playhouse on a wharf, they produced his one-act sea play *Bound East for Cardiff.* The talent inherent in the play was immediately evident to the group, which that fall formed the Playwrights' Theater in Greenwich Village. Their first bill, on Nov. 3, 1916, included *Bound East for Cardiff*—O'Neill's New York debut. Although he was only one of several writers whose plays were produced by the Playwrights' Theater, his contribution within the next few years made the group's reputation. Between 1916 and 1920, the group produced all of O'Neill's one-act sea plays, along with a number of his lesser efforts. By the time his first full-length play, *Beyond the Horizon,* was produced on Broadway, Feb. 2, 1920, at the Morosco Theater, the young playwright already had a small reputation.

Beyond the Horizon impressed the critics with its tragic realism, won for O'Neill the first of four Pulitzer prizes in drama—others were for *Anna Christie, Strange Interlude,* and *Long Day's Journey into Night*—and brought him to the attention of a wider theatre public. For the next 20 years his reputation grew steadily, both in the United States and abroad; after Shakespeare and Shaw, O'Neill became the most widely translated and produced dramatist.

PERIOD OF THE MAJOR WORKS

O'Neill's capacity for and commitment to work were staggering. Between 1920 and 1943 he completed 20 long plays—several of them double and triple length—and a number of shorter ones. He wrote and rewrote many of his manuscripts half a dozen times before he was satisfied, and he filled shelves of notebooks with research notes, outlines, play ideas, and other memoranda. His most distinguished short plays include the four early sea plays, *Bound East for Cardiff, In the Zone, The Long Voyage Home,* and *The Moon of the Caribbees,* which were written between 1913 and 1917 and produced in 1924 under the overall title *S.S. Glencairn; The Emperor Jones* (about the disintegration of a Pullman porter turned tropical-island dictator); and *The Hairy Ape* (about the disintegration of a displaced steamship coal stoker).

O'Neill's plays were written from an intensely personal point of view, deriving directly from the scarring

Paul Robeson as the title character in a 1925 production of Eugene O'Neill's The Emperor Jones. *Sasha/ Hulton Archive/Getty Images*

effects of his family's tragic relationships—his mother and father, who loved and tormented each other; his older brother, who loved and corrupted him and died of alcoholism in middle age; and O'Neill himself, caught and torn between love for and rage at all three.

Among his most-celebrated long plays is *Anna Christie,* perhaps the classic American example of the ancient "harlot with a heart of gold" theme; it became an instant popular success. O'Neill's serious, almost solemn treatment of the struggle of a poor Swedish American girl to live down her early, enforced life of prostitution and to find happiness with a likable but unimaginative young sailor is his least-complicated tragedy. He himself disliked it from the moment he finished it, for, in his words, it had been "too easy."

The first full-length play in which O'Neill successfully evoked the starkness and inevitability of Greek tragedy that he felt in his own life was *Desire Under the Elms* (1924). Drawing on Greek themes of incest, infanticide, and fateful retribution, he framed his story in the context of his own family's conflicts. This story of a lustful father, a weak son, and an adulterous wife who murders her infant son was told with a fine disregard for the conventions of the contemporary Broadway theatre. Because of the sparseness of its style, its avoidance of melodrama, and its total honesty of emotion, the play was acclaimed immediately as a powerful tragedy and has continued to rank among the great American plays of the 20th century.

In *The Great God Brown*, O'Neill dealt with a major theme that he expressed more effectively in later plays—the conflict between idealism and materialism. Although the play was too metaphysically intricate to be staged successfully when it was first produced, in 1926, it was significant for its symbolic use of masks and for the experimentation with expressionistic dialogue and action—devices that since have become commonly accepted both on the stage and in motion pictures. In spite of its confusing structure, the play is rich in symbolism and poetry, as well as in daring technique, and it became a forerunner of avant-garde movements in American theatre.

O'Neill's innovative writing continued with *Strange Interlude*. This play was revolutionary in style and length. When first produced, it opened in late afternoon, broke for a dinner intermission, and ended at the conventional hour. Techniques new to the modern theatre included spoken asides or soliloquies to express the characters' hidden thoughts. The play is the saga of Everywoman, who ritualistically acts out her roles as daughter, wife, mistress, mother, and platonic friend. Although it was innovative and startling in 1928, its obvious Freudian overtones have rapidly dated the work.

One of O'Neill's enduring masterpieces, *Mourning Becomes Electra* (1931), represents the playwright's most complete use of Greek forms, themes, and characters. Based on the *Oresteia* trilogy by Aeschylus, it was itself three plays in one. To give the story contemporary credibility, O'Neill set the play in the New England of the Civil War period, yet he retained the forms and the conflicts of the Greek characters: the heroic leader returning from war; his adulterous wife, who murders him; his jealous, repressed daughter, who avenges him through the murder of her mother; and his weak, incestuous son, who is goaded by his sister first to matricide and then to suicide.

Following a long succession of tragic visions, O'Neill's only comedy, *Ah, Wilderness!,* appeared on Broadway in 1933. Written in a lighthearted, nostalgic mood, the work was inspired in part by the playwright's mischievous desire to demonstrate that he could portray the comic as well as the tragic side of life. Significantly, the play is set in the same place and period, a small New England town in the early 1900s, as his later tragic masterpiece, *Long Day's Journey into Night.* Dealing with the growing pains of a sensitive, adolescent boy, *Ah, Wilderness!* was characterized by O'Neill as "the other side of the coin," meaning that it represented his fantasy of what his own youth might have been, rather than what he believed it to have been (as dramatized later in *Long Day's Journey into Night*).

The Iceman Cometh, the most complex and perhaps the finest of the O'Neill tragedies, followed in 1939, although it did not appear on Broadway until 1946. Laced with subtle religious symbolism, the play is a study of man's need to cling to his hope for a better life, even if he must delude himself to do so.

Even in his last writings, O'Neill's youth continued to absorb his attention. The posthumous production of *Long Day's Journey into Night* brought to light an agonizingly autobiographical play, one of O'Neill's greatest. It is straightforward in style but shattering in its depiction of the agonized relations between father, mother, and two sons. Spanning one day in the life of a family, the play strips away layer after layer from each of the four central figures, revealing the mother as a defeated drug addict, the father as a man frustrated in his career and failed as a husband and father, the older son as a bitter alcoholic, and the younger son as a tubercular, disillusioned youth with only the slenderest chance for physical and spiritual survival.

O'Neill's tragic view of life was perpetuated in his relationships with the three women he married—two of whom he divorced—and his three children. His elder son, Eugene O'Neill, Jr. (by his first wife, Kathleen Jenkins), committed suicide at 40, while his younger son, Shane (by his second wife, Agnes Boulton), drifted into a life of emotional instability. His daughter, Oona (also by Agnes Boulton), was cut out of his life when, at 18, she infuriated him by marrying the film star Charlie Chaplin, who was O'Neill's age.

Until some years after his death in 1953, O'Neill, although respected in the United States, was more highly regarded abroad. Sweden, in particular, always held him in high esteem, partly because of his publicly acknowledged debt to the influence of the Swedish playwright August Strindberg, whose tragic themes often echo in O'Neill's plays. In 1936 the Swedish Academy gave O'Neill the Nobel Prize for Literature, the first time the award had been conferred on an American playwright.

O'Neill's most ambitious project for the theatre was one that he never completed. In the late 1930s he conceived of a cycle of 11 plays, to be performed on 11 consecutive nights, tracing the lives of an American family from the early 1800s to modern times. He wrote scenarios and outlines for several of the plays and drafts of others but completed only one in the cycle—*A Touch of the Poet*—before a crippling illness ended his ability to hold a pencil. An unfinished rough draft of another of the cycle plays, *More Stately Mansions,* was published in 1964 and produced three years later on Broadway, in spite of written instructions left by O'Neill that the incomplete manuscript be destroyed after his death.

O'Neill's final years were spent in grim frustration. Unable to work, he longed for his death and sat waiting for it in a Boston hotel, seeing no one except his doctor, a nurse, and his third wife, Carlotta Monterey. O'Neill died in 1953, as broken and tragic a figure as any he had created for the stage.

ASSESSMENT

O'Neill was the first American dramatist to regard the stage as a literary medium and the only American playwright ever to receive the Nobel Prize for Literature. Through his efforts, the American theatre grew up during the 1920s, developing into a cultural medium that could take its place with the best in American fiction, painting, and music. Until his *Beyond the Horizon* was produced, in 1920, Broadway theatrical fare, apart from musicals and an occasional European import of quality, had consisted largely of contrived melodrama and farce. O'Neill saw the theatre as a valid forum for the presentation of serious ideas. Imbued with the tragic sense of life, he aimed for a contemporary drama that had its roots in the most powerful of ancient Greek tragedies—a drama that could rise to the emotional heights of Shakespeare. For more than 20 years, both with such masterpieces as *Desire Under the Elms, Mourning Becomes Electra,* and *The Iceman Cometh* and by his inspiration to other serious dramatists, O'Neill set the pace for the blossoming of the Broadway theatre.

LILLIAN HELLMAN

No other dramatist was as generally praised as O'Neill, but Lillian Hellman, an American playwright and motion-picture screenwriter, produced distinguished dramas that forcefully attacked injustice, exploitation, and selfishness.

Hellman was born in New Orleans, La., in 1905, but her family soon relocated to New York, where she attended New York public schools and New York University and

Columbia University. Her marriage (1925–32) to the playwright Arthur Kober ended in divorce. She had already begun an intimate friendship with the novelist Dashiell Hammett that would continue until his death in 1961. In the 1930s, after working as book reviewer, press agent, play reader, and Hollywood scenarist, she began writing plays.

Her dramas exposed some of the various forms in which evil appears—a malicious child's lies about two schoolteachers (*The*

Lillian Hellman. Hulton Archive/ Getty Images

Children's Hour, 1934); a ruthless family's exploitation of fellow townspeople and of one another (*The Little Foxes,* 1939, and *Another Part of the Forest,* 1946); and the irresponsible selfishness of the Versailles-treaty generation (*Watch on the Rhine,* 1941, and *The Searching Wind,* 1944). Criticized at times for her doctrinaire views and characters, she nevertheless kept her characters from becoming merely social points of view by writing credible dialogue and creating a realistic intensity matched by few of her playwriting contemporaries. These plays exhibit the tight structure and occasional overcontrivance of what is known as the well-made play. In the 1950s she showed her skill in handling the more subtle structure of Chekhovian drama (*The Autumn Garden,* 1951) and in translating and adapting (Jean Anouilh's *The Lark,* 1955, and Voltaire's *Candide,* 1957, in a musical version). She returned to the well-made play with

Actors Fay Compton and Ronald Ward in a 1942 London production of
Little Foxes. *The drama focuses on avarice and the fight for power within a
wealthy Southern family.* Felix Man/Hulton Archvie/Getty Images

Toys in the Attic (1960), which was followed by another adaptation, *My Mother, My Father, and Me* (1963; from Burt Blechman's novel *How Much?*). She also edited Anton Chekhov's *Selected Letters* (1955) and a collection of stories and short novels, *The Big Knockover* (1966), by Hammett.

Hellman's reminiscences, begun in *An Unfinished Woman* (1969), were continued in *Pentimento* (1973) and *Maybe* (1980). After their publication, certain fabrications were brought to light, notably her reporting in *Pentimento* of a personal relationship with a courageous woman she called Julia. The woman on whose actions Hellman's story was based denied acquaintance with the author.

Hellman, a longtime supporter of leftist causes, detailed in *Scoundrel Time* (1976) her troubles and those of her friends with the House Un-American Activities Committee hearings during the 1950s. Hellman refused to give the committee the names of people who had associations with the Communist Party; she was subsequently blacklisted though not held in contempt of Congress. She remained politically active until her death in 1985.

Her collected plays, many of which continue to be performed today, were published in 1972.

Thornton Wilder

Another noteworthy American dramatist of the early 20th century was Thornton Wilder, whose innovative plays reflect his views of the universal truths in human nature.

Wilder was born in Madison, Wis., in 1897. After graduating from Yale University in 1920, Wilder studied archaeology in Rome. From 1930 to 1937 he taught dramatic literature and the classics at the University of Chicago.

His first novel, *The Cabala* (1926), set in 20th-century Rome, is essentially a fantasy about the death of the pagan gods. His most popular novel, *The Bridge of San Luis Rey* (1927; Pulitzer Prize), which was adapted for film and television, examines the lives of five people who died in the collapse of a bridge in 18th-century Peru. *The Woman of Andros* (1930) is an interpretation of Terence's *Andria*. Accused of being a "Greek" rather than an American writer, Wilder in *Heaven's My Destination* (1934) wrote about a quixotically good hero in a contemporary setting. His later novels are *The Ides of March* (1948), *The Eighth Day* (1967), and *Theophilus North* (1973).

Wilder's plays engage the audience in make-believe by having the actors address the spectators directly and by discarding props and scenery. The Stage Manager in *Our Town* (1938) talks to the audience, as do the characters in the farcical *The Matchmaker* (1954). Wilder won a Pulitzer Prize for *Our Town*, becoming the only person to receive the award in both the fiction and drama categories. *The Matchmaker* was made into a film in 1958 and adapted in 1964 into the immensely successful musical *Hello, Dolly!*, which was also made into a film.

Wilder's other plays include *The Skin of Our Teeth* (1942; Pulitzer Prize), which employs deliberate anachronisms and the use of the same characters in various geological and historical periods to show that human experience is much the same whatever the time or place. Posthumous publications (Wilder died in 1975) include *The Journals of Thornton Wilder, 1939–1961* (1985), edited by Donald Gallup, and Wilder's correspondence with Gertrude Stein, *The Letters of Gertrude Stein and Thornton Wilder* (1996), edited by Edward Burns and Ulla E. Dydo.

OTHER SIGNIFICANT DRAMATISTS OF THE ERA

Many other authors wrote plays that reflected the growth of a serious and varied drama, including Maxwell Anderson, whose verse dramas have dated badly, and Robert E. Sherwood, a Broadway professional who wrote both comedy (*Reunion in Vienna* [1931]) and tragedy (*There Shall Be No Night* [1940]). Marc Connelly wrote touching fantasy in an African American folk biblical play, *The Green Pastures* (1930). Like O'Neill, Elmer Rice made use of both Expressionistic techniques (*The Adding Machine* [1923]) and naturalism (*Street Scene* [1929]).

Radical theatre experiments included Marc Blitzstein's savagely satiric musical *The Cradle Will Rock* (1937) and the

Clifford Odets

(b. July 18, 1906, Philadelphia, Pa., U.S.—d. Aug. 14, 1963, Hollywood, Calif.)

Clifford Odets was a leading dramatist of the theatre of social protest in the United States during the 1930s. His important affiliation with the celebrated Group Theatre contributed to that company's considerable influence on the American stage.

From 1923 to 1928 Odets learned his profession as an actor in repertory companies; in 1931 he joined the newly founded Group Theatre as one of its original members. Odets's *Waiting for Lefty* (1935), his first great success, used both auditorium and stage for action and was an effective plea for labour unionism; *Awake and Sing* (1935) is a naturalistic family drama; and *Golden Boy* (1937; filmed 1939) concerns an Italian youth who rejects his artistic potential to become a boxer. *Paradise Lost* (1935) deals with the tragic life of a middle-class family. In 1936 Odets married the Austrian actress Luise Rainer.

Odets moved to Hollywood in the late '30s to write for motion pictures and became a successful director. His later plays include *The Big Knife* (1949), *The Country Girl* (1950; U.K. title *Winter Journey*), and *The Flowering Peach* (1954).

work of Orson Welles and John Houseman for the government-sponsored Works Progress Administration (WPA) Federal Theatre Project. The premier radical theatre of the decade was the Group Theatre (1931–41) under Harold Clurman and Lee Strasberg, which became best known for presenting the work of Clifford Odets. In *Waiting for Lefty* (1935), a stirring plea for labour unionism, Odets roused the audience to an intense pitch of fervour, and in *Awake and Sing* (1935), perhaps the best play of the decade, he created a lyrical work of family conflict and youthful yearning. Other important plays by Odets for the Group Theatre were *Paradise Lost* (1935), *Golden Boy* (1937), and *Rocket to the Moon* (1938). William Saroyan shifted his light-hearted, anarchic vision from fiction to drama with *My Heart's in the Highlands* and *The Time of Your Life* (both 1939).

THE NEW POETRY

Poetry in the early 20th century ranged between traditional types of verse and experimental writing that departed radically from the established forms of the 19th century. Two New England poets not noted for technical experimentation, Edwin Arlington Robinson and Robert Frost, won both critical and popular acclaim in this period. Robinson, whose first book appeared in 1896, did his best work in sonnets, ballad stanzas, and blank verse. In the 1920s he won three Pulitzer Prizes—for his *Collected Poems* (published 1921), *The Man Who Died Twice* (1925), and *Tristram* (1927). Like Robinson, Frost used traditional stanzas and blank verse in volumes such as *A Boy's Will* (1913), his first book, and *North of Boston* (1914), *New Hampshire* (1923), *A Further Range* (1936), and *A Masque of Reason* (1945). The best-known poet of his generation, Frost, like Robinson, saw and commented upon the tragic aspects of life in poems such as "Design,"

"Directive," and "Provide, Provide." Frost memorably crafted the language of common speech into traditional poetic form, with epigrammatic effect.

Just as modern American drama had its beginnings in little theatres, modern American poetry took form in little magazines. Particularly important was *Poetry: A Magazine of Verse*, founded by Harriet Monroe in Chicago in 1912. The surrounding region soon became prominent as the home of three poets: Vachel Lindsay, Carl Sandburg, and Edgar Lee Masters. Lindsay's blend of legendary lore and native oratory in irregular odelike forms was well adapted to oral presentation, and his lively readings from his works contributed to the success of such books as *General William Booth Enters into Heaven, and Other Poems* (1913) and *The Congo, and Other Poems* (1914). Sandburg wrote of life on the prairies and in Midwestern cities in Whitmanesque free verse in such volumes as *Chicago Poems* (1916) and *The People, Yes* (1936). Masters's very popular *Spoon River Anthology* (1915) consisted of free-verse monologues by village men and women, most of whom spoke bitterly of their frustrated lives.

Writing traditional sonnets and brief, personal lyrics, Edna St. Vincent Millay and Sara Teasdale were innovative in being unusually frank (according to the standard of their time) for women poets. Amy Lowell, on the other hand, experimented with free verse and focused on the image and the descriptive detail. Three fine black poets— James Weldon Johnson, Langston Hughes, and Countee Cullen—found old molds satisfactory for dealing with new subjects, specifically the problems of racism in America. The deceptively simple colloquial language of Hughes's poetry has proved especially appealing to later readers. While Conrad Aiken experimented with poetical imitations of symphonic forms often mingled with stream-of-consciousness techniques, E.E. Cummings used typographical novelties to produce poems that had surprisingly fresh impact. Marianne Moore invented and brilliantly employed a kind of free verse that was marked by a wonderfully sharp and idiosyncratic focus on objects and details. Robinson Jeffers used violent imagery and modified free or blank verse to express perhaps the most bitter views voiced by a major poet in this period.

Except for a period after World War II, when he was confined in St. Elizabeth's Hospital in Washington, D.C., Ezra Pound lived outside the United States after 1908. He had, nevertheless, a profound influence on 20th-century writing in English, both as a practitioner of verse and as a patron and impresario of other writers. His most controversial work remained *The Cantos*, the first installment of which appeared in 1926 and the latest in 1959 (*Thrones: 96–109 de los cantares*), with a fragmentary addendum in 1968 (*Drafts & Fragments of Cantos CX–CXVII*).

Like Pound, to whom he was much indebted, T.S. Eliot lived abroad most of his life, becoming a British subject in 1927. His first volume, *Prufrock and Other Observations*, was published in 1917. In 1922 appeared *The Waste Land*, the poem by which he first became famous. Filled with fragments, competing voices, learned allusions, and deeply buried personal details, the poem was read as a dark diagnosis of a disillusioned generation and of the modern world. As a poet and critic, Eliot exercised a strong influence, especially in the period between World Wars I and II. In what some critics regard as his finest work, *Four Quartets* (1943), Eliot explored through images of great beauty and haunting power his own past, the past of the human race, and the meaning of human history.

Eliot was an acknowledged master of a varied group of poets whose work was indebted to 17th-century English Metaphysical poets, especially to John Donne. Eliot's influence was clear in the writings of Archibald MacLeish, whose earlier poems showed resemblances to *The Waste Land*. A number of Southern poets (who were also critics) were influenced by Eliot—John Crowe Ransom, Donald Davidson, and Allen Tate. Younger American Metaphysicals who emerged later included Louise Bogan, Léonie Adams, Muriel Rukeyser, Delmore Schwartz, and Karl Shapiro. But there were several major poets strongly opposed to Eliot's influence. Their style and subjects tended to be romantic and visionary. These included Hart Crane, whose long poem *The Bridge* (1930) aimed to create a Whitmanesque American epic, and Wallace Stevens, a lush and sensuous writer who made an astonishing literary debut with the poems collected in *Harmonium* (1923). Another opponent of Eliot was William Carlos Williams, who invested his experimental prose and magically simple lyrics—in works such as *Spring and All* (1923)—with the mundane details of American life and wrote about American myth and cultural history with great sweep in *In the American Grain* (1925).

ROBERT FROST

(b. March 26, 1874, San Francisco, Calif., U.S.—d. Jan. 29, 1963, Boston, Mass.)

The American poet Robert Frost was much admired for his depictions of the rural life of New England, his command of American colloquial speech, and his realistic verse portraying ordinary people in everyday situations.

LIFE

Frost's father, William Prescott Frost, Jr., was a journalist with ambitions of establishing a career in California, and in 1873 he and his wife moved to San Francisco. Her husband's untimely death from tuberculosis in 1885 prompted Isabelle Moodie Frost to take her two children, Robert and Jeanie, to Lawrence, Mass., where they were taken in by the children's paternal grandparents. While their mother taught at a variety of schools in New Hampshire and Massachusetts, Robert and Jeanie grew up in Lawrence, and Robert graduated from high school in 1892. A top student in his class, he shared valedictorian honours with Elinor White, with whom he had already fallen in love.

Robert and Elinor shared a deep interest in poetry, but their continued education sent Robert to Dartmouth College and Elinor to St. Lawrence University. Meanwhile, Robert continued to labour on the poetic career he had begun in a small way during high school; he first achieved professional publication in 1894 when *The Independent*, a weekly literary journal, printed his poem "My Butterfly: An Elegy." Impatient with academic routine, Frost left Dartmouth after less than a year. He and Elinor married in 1895 but found life difficult, and the young poet supported them by teaching school and farming, neither with notable success. During the next dozen years, six children were born, two of whom died early, leaving a family of one son and three daughters. Frost resumed his college education at Harvard University in 1897 but left after two years' study there. From 1900 to 1909 the family raised poultry on a farm near Derry, N.H., and for a time Frost also taught at the Pinkerton Academy in Derry. Frost became an enthusiastic botanist and acquired his poetic persona of a New England rural sage during the years he and his family spent at Derry. All this while he was writing poems, but publishing outlets showed little interest in them.

By 1911 Frost was fighting against discouragement. Poetry had always been considered a young person's game, but Frost, who was nearly 40 years old, had not published a single book of poems and had seen just a handful appear in magazines. In 1911 ownership of the Derry farm passed to Frost. A momentous decision was made: to sell the farm and use the proceeds to make a radical new start in London, where publishers were perceived to be more receptive to new talent. Accordingly, in August 1912 the Frost family sailed across the Atlantic to England. Frost carried with him sheaves of verses he had written but not gotten into print. English publishers in London did indeed prove more receptive to innovative verse, and, through his own vigorous efforts and those of the expatriate American poet Ezra Pound, Frost within a year had published *A Boy's Will* (1913). From this first book, such poems as "Storm Fear," "Mowing," and "The Tuft of Flowers" have remained standard anthology pieces.

A Boy's Will was followed in 1914 by a second collection, *North of Boston*, that introduced some of the most popular poems in all of Frost's work, among them "Mending Wall," "The Death of the Hired Man," "Home Burial," and "After Apple-Picking." In London, Frost's name was frequently mentioned by those who followed the course of modern literature, and soon American visitors were returning home with news of this unknown poet who was causing a sensation abroad. The Boston poet Amy Lowell traveled to England in 1914, and in the bookstores there she encountered Frost's work. Taking his books home to America, Lowell then began a campaign to locate an American publisher for them, meanwhile writing her own laudatory review of *North of Boston*.

Without his being fully aware of it, Frost was on his way to fame. The outbreak of World War I brought the Frosts back to the United States in 1915. By then Amy Lowell's review had already appeared in *The New Republic*, and writers and publishers throughout the Northeast were aware that a writer of unusual abilities stood in their midst. The American publishing house of Henry Holt had brought out its edition of *North of Boston* in 1914. It became

Robert Frost, 1954. Ruohomaa/Black Star

a best-seller, and, by the time the Frost family landed in Boston, Holt was adding the American edition of *A Boy's Will.* Frost soon found himself besieged by magazines seeking to publish his poems. Never before had an American poet achieved such rapid fame after such a disheartening delay. From this moment his career rose on an ascending curve.

Frost bought a small farm at Franconia, N.H., in 1915, but his income from both poetry and farming proved inadequate to support his family, and so he lectured and taught part-time at Amherst College and at the University of Michigan from 1916 to 1938. Any remaining doubt about his poetic abilities was dispelled by the collection *Mountain Interval* (1916), which continued the high level established by his first books. His reputation was further enhanced by *New Hampshire* (1923), which received the Pulitzer Prize. That prize was also awarded to Frost's *Collected Poems* (1930) and to the collections *A Further Range* (1936) and *A Witness Tree* (1942). His other poetry volumes include *West-Running Brook* (1928), *Steeple Bush* (1947), and *In the Clearing* (1962). Frost served as a poet-in-residence at Harvard (1939–43), Dartmouth (1943–49), and Amherst College (1949–63), and in his old age he gathered honours and awards from every quarter. He was the poetry consultant to the Library of Congress (1958–59; the post is now styled poet laureate consultant in poetry), and his recital of his poem "The Gift Outright" at the inauguration of President John F. Kennedy in 1961 was a memorable occasion.

WORKS

The poems in Frost's early books, especially *North of Boston*, differ radically from late 19th-century Romantic verse with its ever-benign view of nature, its didactic emphasis, and its slavish conformity to established verse forms and themes. Lowell called *North of Boston* a "sad" book, referring to its portraits of inbred, isolated, and psychologically troubled rural New Englanders. These off-mainstream portraits signaled Frost's departure from the old tradition and his own fresh interest in delineating New England characters and their formative background. Among these psychological investigations are the alienated life of Silas in "The Death of the Hired Man," the inability of Amy in "Home Burial" to walk the difficult path from grief back to normality, the rigid mind-set of the neighbour in "Mending Wall," and the paralyzing fear that twists the personality of Doctor Magoon in "A Hundred Collars."

The natural world, for Frost, wore two faces. Early on he overturned the Emersonian concept of nature as healer and mentor in a poem in *A Boy's Will* entitled "Storm Fear," a grim picture of a blizzard as a raging beast that dares the inhabitants of an isolated house to come outside and be killed. In such later poems as "The Hill Wife" and "Stopping by Woods on a Snowy Evening," the benign surface of nature cloaks potential dangers, and death itself lurks behind dark, mysterious trees. Nature's frolicsome aspect predominates in other poems such as "Birches," where a destructive ice storm is recalled as a thing of memorable beauty. Although Frost is known to many as essentially a "happy" poet, the tragic elements in life continued to mark his poems, from "'Out, Out—'" (1916), in which a lad's hand is severed and life ended, to a fine verse entitled "The Fear of Man" from *Steeple Bush*, in which human release from pervading fear is contained in the image of a breathless dash through the nighttime city from the security of one faint street lamp to another just as faint. Even in his final volume, *In the Clearing*, so filled with the stubborn courage of old age, Frost portrays human security as a rather tiny and quite vulnerable opening in a thickly grown forest, a pinpoint of light against which the encroaching trees cast their very real threat of darkness.

Frost demonstrated an enviable versatility of theme, but he most commonly investigated human contacts with the natural world in small encounters that serve as metaphors for larger aspects of the human condition. He often portrayed the human ability to turn even the slightest incident or natural detail to emotional profit, seen at its most economical form in "Dust of Snow":

The way a crow
Shook down on me
The dust of snow
From a hemlock tree
Has given my heart
A change of mood
And saved some part
Of a day I had rued.

Other poems are portraits of the introspective mind possessed by its own private demons, as in "Desert Places," which could serve to illustrate Frost's celebrated definition of poetry as a "momentary stay against confusion":

They cannot scare me with their empty spaces
Between stars—on stars where no human race is.
I have it in me so much nearer home
To scare myself with my own desert places.

Frost was widely admired for his mastery of metrical form, which he often set against the natural rhythms of everyday, unadorned speech. In this way the traditional stanza and metrical line achieved new vigour in his hands. Frost's command of traditional metrics is evident in the tight, older, prescribed patterns of such sonnets as "Design" and "The Silken Tent." His strongest allegiance probably was to the quatrain with simple rhymes such as *abab* and *abcb*, and within its restrictions he was able to achieve an infinite variety, as in the aforementioned "Dust of Snow" and "Desert Places." Frost was never an enthusi-ast of free verse and regarded its looseness as something less than ideal, similar to playing tennis without a net. His determination to be "new" but to employ "old ways to be new" set him aside from the radical experimentalism of the advocates of vers libre in the early 20th century. On occasion Frost did employ free verse to advantage, one outstanding example being "After Apple-Picking," with its random pattern of long and short lines and its nontradi-tional use of rhyme. Here he shows his power to stand as a transitional figure between the old and the new in poetry. Frost mastered blank verse (i.e., unrhymed verse in iambic pentameter) for use in such dramatic narratives as "Mending Wall" and "Home Burial," becoming one of the few modern poets to use it both appropriately and well. His chief technical innovation in these dramatic-dialogue poems was to unify the regular pentameter line with the irregular rhythms of conversational speech. Frost's blank verse has the same terseness and concision that mark his poetry in general.

ASSESSMENT

Frost was the most widely admired and highly honoured American poet of the 20th century. Amy Lowell thought he had overstressed the dark aspects of New England life, but Frost's later flood of more uniformly optimistic verses made that view seem antiquated. Louis Untermeyer's judgment that the dramatic poems in *North of Boston* were the most authentic and powerful of their kind ever pro-duced by an American has only been confirmed by later opinions. Gradually, Frost's name ceased to be linked solely with New England, and he gained broad acceptance as a national poet.

It is true that certain criticisms of Frost have never been wholly refuted, one being that he was overly interested in the past, another that he was too little concerned with the present and future of American society. Those who criticize Frost's detachment from the "modern" emphasize the undeniable absence in his poems of meaningful references to the modern realities of industrialization, urbanization, and the concentration of wealth, or to such familiar items as radios, motion pictures, automobiles, factories, or skyscrapers. The poet has been viewed as a singer of sweet nostalgia and a social and political conservative who was content to sigh for the good things of the past.

Such views have failed to gain general acceptance, however, in the face of the universality of Frost's themes, the emotional authenticity of his voice, and the austere technical brilliance of his verse. Frost was often able to endow his rural imagery with a larger symbolic or metaphysical significance, and his best poems transcend the immediate realities of their subject matter to illuminate the unique blend of tragic endurance, stoicism, and tenacious affirmation that marked his outlook on life. Over his long career Frost succeeded in lodging more than a few poems where, as he put it, they would be "hard to get rid of," and he can be said to have lodged himself just as solidly in the affections of his fellow Americans. For thousands he remains the only recent poet worth reading and the only one who matters.

CARL SANDBURG

(b. Jan. 6, 1878, Galesburg, Ill., U.S. — d. July 22, 1967, Flat Rock, N.C.)

Carl Sandburg was an American poet, historian, novelist, and folklorist.

From the age of 11, Sandburg worked in various occupations — as a barbershop porter, a milk truck driver, a brickyard hand, and a harvester in the Kansas wheat fields. When the Spanish-American War broke out in 1898, he enlisted in the 6th Illinois Infantry. These early years he later described in his autobiography *Always the Young Strangers* (1953).

From 1910 to 1912 he acted as an organizer for the Social Democratic Party and secretary to the mayor of Milwaukee. Moving to Chicago in 1913, he became an editor of *System,* a business magazine, and later joined the staff of the *Chicago Daily News.*

In 1914 a selection from his *Chicago Poems* appeared in *Poetry* magazine (issued in book form in 1916). In his most famous poem, "Chicago," he depicted the city as the laughing, lusty, heedless "Hog Butcher, Tool Maker, Stacker of Wheat, Player with Railroads and Freight Handler to the Nation." Sandburg's poetry made an instant and favourable impression. In Whitmanesque free verse, he eulogized workers: "Pittsburgh, Youngstown, Gary, they make their steel with men" (*Smoke and Steel,* 1920).

In *Good Morning, America* (1928) Sandburg seemed to have lost some of his faith in democracy, but from the depths of the Great Depression he wrote a poetic testament to the power of the people to go forward, *The People, Yes* (1936). The folk songs he sang before delighted audiences were issued in two collections, *The American Songbag* (1927) and *New American Songbag* (1950). He wrote the popular biography *Abraham Lincoln: The Prairie Years,* 2 vol. (1926), and *Abraham Lincoln: The War Years,* 4 vol. (1939; Pulitzer Prize in history, 1940).

Another biography, *Steichen the Photographer,* the life of his famous brother-in-law, Edward Steichen, appeared in 1929. In 1948 Sandburg published a long novel, *Remembrance Rock,* which recapitulates the American experience from Plymouth Rock to World War II. *Complete Poems* appeared in 1950. He wrote four books for children—*Rootabaga*

Stories (1922); *Rootabaga Pigeons* (1923); *Rootabaga Country* (1929); and *Potato Face* (1930).

Carl Sandburg: "Chicago"

The son of Swedish immigrants, Carl Sandburg had little formal education. After enlisting in the 6th Illinois Infantry during the Spanish-American War, he was sent to Puerto Rico for eight months. There he became close friends with a student at Lombard College, in Sandburg's hometown of Galesburg, Ill., and returned after the war to attend the college. His interest in poetry grew, and he began to write verse.

In 1914, *Poetry: A Magazine of Verse* published several of his poems, including "Chicago," and he was on his way. The description of Chicago has seemed apt to many readers, and Chicagoans themselves are likely to say that their city is still "Stormy, husky, brawling," and that the Midwestern metropolis remains the "City of the Big Shoulders."

This poem is taken from *Poetry*, Chicago, March 1914, p. 191.

Hog Butcher for the World,
Tool Maker, Stacker of Wheat,
Player with Railroads and the Nation's Freight Handler;
Stormy, husky, brawling,
City of the Big Shoulders:

They tell me you are wicked and I believe them, for I have
    seen your painted women under the gas lamps luring the
    farm boys.
And they tell me you are crooked and I answer: Yes, it is true I
    have seen the gunman kill and go free to kill again.
And they tell me you are brutal and my reply is: On the faces of
    women and children I have seen the marks of wanton hunger.
And having answered so I turn once more to those who sneer at
    this my city, and I give them back the sneer and say to them:

Come and show me another city with lifted head singing so
   proud to be alive and coarse and strong and cunning.
Flinging magnetic curses amid the toil of piling job on job, here
   is a tall bold slugger set vivid against the little soft cities;
Fierce as a dog with tongue lapping for action, cunning as a sav-
   age pitted against the wilderness,
                    Bareheaded,
                    Shoveling,
                    Wrecking,
                    Planning,
                    Building, breaking, rebuilding,
Under the smoke, dust all over his mouth, laughing with
   white teeth,
Under the terrible burden of destiny laughing as a young man
   laughs,
Laughing even as an ignorant fighter laughs who has never lost
   a battle,
Bragging and laughing that under his wrist is the pulse, and
   under his ribs the heart of the people, Laughing!
Laughing the stormy, husky, brawling laughter of Youth, half-
   naked, sweating, proud to be Hog Butcher, Tool Maker,
   Stacker of Wheat, Player with Railroads and Freight
   Handler to the Nation.

LANGSTON HUGHES

(b. Feb. 1, 1902, Joplin, Mo., U.S. — d. May 22, 1967, New York, N.Y.)

The poet and writer Langston Hughes became, through numerous translations, one of the foremost interpreters to the world of the black experience in the United States. Hughes's parents separated soon after his birth, and young Hughes was raised by his mother and grandmother. After his grandmother's death, he and his mother moved to half a dozen cities before reaching Cleveland, where they settled. His poem "The Negro Speaks of Rivers," written the summer after his graduation from high school in Cleveland, was published in *The Crisis* (1921) and brought him considerable attention.

After attending Columbia University (1921–22), he explored Harlem, forming a permanent attachment to what he called the "great dark city." He worked as a steward on a freighter bound for Africa. Back from seafaring and sojourning in Europe, he won an *Opportunity* magazine poetry prize in 1925. He received the Witter Bynner Undergraduate Poetry Award in 1926.

While working as a busboy in a hotel in Washington, D.C., Hughes put three of his own poems beside the plate of Vachel Lindsay in the dining room. The next day, newspapers around the country reported that Lindsay had discovered an African American busboy poet. A scholarship to Lincoln University in Pennsylvania followed, and before Hughes received his degree in 1929, his first two books had been published.

The Weary Blues (1926) was warmly received. *Fine Clothes to the Jew* (1927) was criticized harshly for its title and for its frankness, but Hughes himself felt it represented a step forward. A few months after graduation *Not Without Laughter* (1930), his first prose work, had a cordial reception. In the '30s his poetry became preoccupied with political militancy; he traveled widely in the Soviet Union, Haiti, and Japan and served as a newspaper correspondent (1937) in the Spanish Civil War. He published a collection of short stories, *The Ways of White Folks* (1934), and *The Big Sea* (1940), his autobiography up to age 28.

Hughes wrote *A Pictorial History of the Negro in America* (1956), and the anthologies *The Poetry of the Negro* (1949) and *The Book of Negro Folklore* (1958; with Arna Bontemps). He also wrote numerous works for the stage, including the lyrics for *Street Scene*, an opera with music by Kurt Weill. A posthumous book of poems, *The Panther and the Lash* (1967), reflected the black anger and militancy of the

Although Langston Hughes, pictured c. 1944, wrote prose and works for the stage, he is considered first and foremost a poet. In all formats, Hughes examined the black experience in America. Hulton Archive/Getty Images

1960s. Hughes translated the poetry of Federico García Lorca and Gabriela Mistral. He was also widely known for his comic character Jesse B. Semple, familiarly called Simple, who appeared in Hughes's columns in the *Chicago Defender* and the *New York Post* and later in book form and on the stage. *The Collected Poems of Langston Hughes*, ed. by Arnold Rampersad and David Roessel, appeared in 1994.

E.E. CUMMINGS
(b. Oct. 14, 1894, Cambridge, Mass., U.S.—d. Sept. 3, 1962, North Conway, N.H.)

E.E. Cummings was an American poet and painter who first attracted attention, in an age of literary experimentation, for his eccentric punctuation and phrasing. The spirit of New England dissent and of Emersonian "Self-Reliance" underlies the urbanized Yankee colloquialism of Cummings's verse. Cummings's name is often styled "e.e. cummings" in the mistaken belief that the poet legally changed his name to lowercase letters only. Cummings used capital letters only irregularly in his verse and did not object when publishers began lowercasing his name, but he himself capitalized his name in his signature and in the title pages of original editions of his books.

Edward Estlin Cummings received his B.A. degree from Harvard University in 1915 and was awarded his M.A. in 1916. During World War I he served with an ambulance corps in France, where he was interned for a time in a detention camp because of his friendship with an American who had written letters home that the French censors thought critical of the war effort. This experience deepened Cummings's distrust of officialdom and was symbolically recounted in his first book, *The Enormous Room* (1922).

In the 1920s and '30s he divided his time between Paris, where he studied art, and New York City. His first book of verse was *Tulips and Chimneys* (1923), followed by *XLI Poems* and *&* (1925); in the latter year he received the Dial award for distinguished service to American letters.

In 1927 his play *him* was produced by the Provincetown Players in New York City. During these years he exhibited his paintings and drawings, but they failed to attract as much critical interest as his writings. *Eimi* (1933) recorded, in 432 pages of experimental prose, a 36-day visit to the Soviet Union, which confirmed his individualist repugnance for collectivism. He published his discussions as the Charles Eliot Norton lecturer on poetry at Harvard University (1952–53) under the title *i: six nonlectures* (1953).

In all he wrote 12 volumes of verse, assembled in his two-volume *Complete Poems* (1968). Cummings's moods were alternately satirical and tough or tender and whimsical. He frequently used the language of the streets and material from burlesque and the circus. His erotic poetry and love lyrics had a childlike candour and freshness.

MARIANNE MOORE

(b. Nov. 15, 1887, St. Louis, Mo., U.S.—d. Feb. 5, 1972, New York, N.Y.)

Marianne Moore was an American poet whose work distilled moral and intellectual insights from the close and accurate observation of objective detail.

Moore graduated from Bryn Mawr College in Pennsylvania in 1909 as a biology major and then studied commercial subjects and taught them at the U.S. Indian School in Carlisle, Pa. Her first published work appeared in 1915 in the *Egoist* and in Harriet Monroe's *Poetry* magazine. After 1919, living in Brooklyn, N.Y., with her mother, Moore devoted herself to writing, contributing poetry and criticism to many journals in the United States and England.

In 1921 her first book, *Poems*, was published in London by Hilda Doolittle and Winifred Ellerman (byname Bryher). Her first American volume was titled *Observations* (1924). These initial collections exhibited Moore's conciseness and her ability to create a mosaic of juxtaposed images that lead unerringly to a conclusion that, at its best, is both surprising and inevitable. They contain some of her best-known poems, including "To a Steam Roller," "The Fish," "When I Buy Pictures," "Peter," "The Labors of Hercules," and "Poetry." The last named is the source of her often-quoted admonition that poets should present imaginary gardens with real toads in them.

In 1925—already well known as one of the leading new poets—she became acting editor of *The Dial*, an influential American journal of literature and arts, and she remained with *The Dial* until it was discontinued in 1929. Moore's *Collected Poems* appeared in 1951. She also published a translation of *The Fables of La Fontaine* (1954); a volume of critical papers, *Predilections* (1955); and *Idiosyncrasy and Technique: Two Lectures* (1958).

A disciplined craftsman, Moore won the admiration of fellow poets throughout her long career. The poet and critic T.S. Eliot called her one of the few producers of durable poetry in her time.

EZRA POUND

(b. Oct. 30, 1885, Hailey, Idaho, U.S.—d. Nov. 1, 1972, Venice, Italy)

The American poet and critic Ezra Pound was a supremely discerning and energetic entrepreneur of the arts who did more than any other single figure to advance a "modern" movement in English and American literature. Pound promoted, and also occasionally helped to shape, the work of such widely different poets and novelists as William Butler Yeats, James Joyce, Ernest Hemingway, Robert Frost, D.H. Lawrence, and T.S. Eliot. His pro-Fascist broadcasts in Italy during World War II led to his postwar arrest and confinement until 1958.

EARLY LIFE AND CAREER

Pound was born in a small mining town in Idaho, the only child of a Federal Land Office official, Homer Loomis Pound of Wisconsin, and Isabel Weston of New York City. About 1887 the family moved to the eastern states, and in June 1889, following Homer Pound's appointment to the U.S. Mint in Philadelphia, they settled in nearby Wyncote, where Pound lived a normal middle-class childhood.

After two years at Cheltenham Military Academy, which he left without graduating, he attended a local high school. From there he went for two years (1901–03) to the University of Pennsylvania, where he met his lifelong friend, the poet William Carlos Williams. He took a Ph.B. (bachelor of philosophy) degree at Hamilton College, Clinton, N.Y., in 1905 and returned to the University of Pennsylvania for graduate work. He received his M.A. in June 1906 but withdrew from the university after working one more year toward his doctorate. He left with a knowledge of Latin, Greek, French, Italian, German, Spanish, Provençal, and Anglo-Saxon, as well as of English literature and grammar.

In the autumn of 1907, Pound became professor of Romance languages at Wabash Presbyterian College, Crawfordsville, Ind. Although his general behaviour fairly reflected his Presbyterian upbringing, he was already writing poetry and was affecting a bohemian manner. His career came quickly to an end, and in February 1908, with light luggage and the manuscript of a book of poems that had been rejected by at least one American publisher, he set sail for Europe.

He had been to Europe three times before, the third time alone in the summer of 1906, when he had gathered the material for his first three published articles: "Raphaelite Latin," concerning the Latin poets of the Renaissance, and "Interesting French Publications," concerning the troubadours (both published in the *Book News Monthly*, Philadelphia, September 1906), and "Burgos, a Dream City of Old Castile" (October issue).

Now, with little money, he sailed to Gibraltar and southern Spain, then on to Venice, where in June 1908 he published, at his own expense, his first book of poems, *A lume spento*. About September 1908 he went to London, where he was befriended by the writer and editor Ford Madox Ford (who published him in his *English Review*), entered William Butler Yeats's circle, and joined the "school of images," a modern group presided over by the philosopher T.E. Hulme.

SUCCESS ABROAD

In England, success came quickly to Pound. A book of poems, *Personae*, was published in April 1909; a second book, *Exultations*, followed in October; and a third book, *The Spirit of Romance*, based on lectures delivered in London (1909–10), was published in 1910.

After a trip home—a last desperate and unsuccessful attempt to make a literary life for himself in Philadelphia or New York City—he returned to Europe in February 1911, visiting Italy, Germany, and France. Toward the end of 1911 he met an English journalist, Alfred R. Orage, editor of the socialist weekly *New Age*, who opened its pages to him and provided him with a small but regular income during the next nine years.

In 1912 Pound became London correspondent for the small magazine *Poetry* (Chicago); he did much to enhance the magazine's importance and was soon a dominant figure in Anglo-American verse. He was among the first to recognize and review the poetry of Robert Frost and D.H. Lawrence and to praise the sculpture of the modernists Jacob Epstein and Henri Gaudier-Brzeska. As leader of the Imagist movement of 1912–14, successor of the "school of images," he drew up the first Imagist manifesto, with its emphasis on direct and sparse language and precise images in poetry, and he edited the first Imagist anthology, *Des Imagistes* (1914).

A SHAPER OF MODERN LITERATURE

Though his friend Yeats had already become famous, Pound succeeded in persuading him to adopt a new, leaner

A published poet himself, Ezra Pound helped shape the landscape of American poetry and prose during the early 20th century as a critic and editor. Hulton Archive/Getty Images

style of poetic composition. In 1914, the year of his marriage to Dorothy Shakespear, daughter of Yeats's friend Olivia Shakespear, he began a collaboration with the then-unknown James Joyce. As unofficial editor of *The Egoist* (London) and later as London editor of the *Little Review* (New York City), he saw to the publication of Joyce's novels *Portrait of the Artist as a Young Man* and *Ulysses*, thus spreading Joyce's name and securing financial assistance for him. In that same year he gave T.S. Eliot a similar start in his career as poet and critic.

He continued to publish his own poetry (*Ripostes*, 1912; *Lustra*, 1916) and prose criticism (*Pavannes and Divisions*, 1918). From the literary remains of the great Orientalist Ernest Fenollosa, which had been presented to Pound in

1913, he succeeded in publishing highly acclaimed English versions of early Chinese poetry, *Cathay* (1915), and two volumes of Japanese Noh plays (1916–17) as well.

DEVELOPMENT AS A POET

Unsettled by the slaughter of World War I and the spirit of hopelessness he felt was pervading England after its conclusion, Pound decided to move to Paris, publishing before he left two of his most important poetical works, "Homage to Sextus Propertius," in the book *Quia Pauper Amavi* (1919), and *Hugh Selwyn Mauberley* (1920). "Propertius" is a comment on the British Empire in 1917, by way of Propertius and the Roman Empire. *Mauberley*, a finely chiseled "portrait" of one aspect of British literary culture in 1919, is one of the most praised poems of the 20th century.

During his 12 years in London, Pound had completely transformed himself as a poet. He arrived a Late Victorian for whom love was a matter of "lute strings," "crushed lips," and "Dim tales that blind me." Within five or six years he was writing a new, adult poetry that spoke calmly of current concerns in common speech. In this drier intellectual air, "as clear as metal," Pound's verse took on new qualities of economy, brevity, and clarity as he used concrete details and exact visual images to capture concentrated moments of experience. Pound's search for laconic precision owed much to his constant reading of past literature, including Anglo-Saxon poetry, Greek and Latin classics, Dante, and such 19th-century French works as Théophile Gautier's *Émaux et camées* and Gustave Flaubert's novel *Madame Bovary*. Like his friend T.S. Eliot, Pound wanted a modernism that brought back to life the highest standards of the past. Modernism for its own sake, untested against the past, drew anathemas from him. His progress may be seen in attempts at informality (1911):

Have tea, damn the Caesars,
Talk of the latest success. . .

in the gathering strength of his 1911 version of the Anglo-Saxon poem "Seafarer":

Storms, on the stone-cliffs beaten,
fell on the stern
In icy feathers. . .

and in the confident free verse of "The Return" (1912):

See, they return; ah, see the tentative
Movements, and the slow feet. . .

From this struggle there emerged the short, perfectly worded free-verse poems in *Lustra*. In his poetry Pound was now able to deal efficiently with a whole range of human activities and emotions, without raising his voice. The movement of the words and the images they create are no longer the secondhand borrowings of youth or apprenticeship but seem to belong to the observing intelligence that conjures up the particular work in hand. Many of the *Lustra* poems are remarkable for perfectly paced endings:

Nor has life in it aught better
Than this hour of clear coolness,
the hour of waking together.

But the culmination of Pound's years in London was his 18-part long poem *Hugh Selwyn Mauberley*, which ranged from close observation of the artist and society to the horrors of mass production and World War I; from brilliant echo of the past:

When our two dusts with Waller's shall be laid,
Siftings on siftings in oblivion,
Till change hath broken down
All things save Beauty alone.

to the syncopation of:

With a placid and uneducated mistress
He exercises his talents
And the soil meets his distress.

THE CANTOS

During his stay in Paris (1921–24) Pound met and helped the young American novelist Ernest Hemingway; wrote an opera, *Le Testament*, based on poems of François Villon; assisted T.S. Eliot with the editing of his long poem *The Waste Land*; and acted as correspondent for the New York literary journal *The Dial*.

In 1924 Pound tired of Paris and moved to Rapallo, Italy, which was to be his home for the next 20 years. In 1925 he had a daughter, Maria, by the expatriate American violinist Olga Rudge, and in 1926 his wife, Dorothy, gave birth to a son, Omar. The daughter was brought up by a peasant woman in the Italian Tirol, the son by relatives in England. In 1927–28 Pound edited his own magazine, *Exile*, and in 1930 he brought together, under the title *A Draft of XXX Cantos*, various segments of his ambitious long poem *The Cantos*, which he had begun in 1915.

The 1930s saw the publication of further volumes of *The Cantos* (*Eleven New Cantos*, 1934; *The Fifth Decad of Cantos*, 1937; *Cantos LII–LXXI*, 1940) and a collection of some of his best prose (*Make It New*, 1934). A growing interest in music caused him to arrange a long series of concerts in Rapallo during the 1930s, and, with the assistance of Olga Rudge, he played a large part in the rediscovery of the 18th-century Italian composer Antonio Vivaldi. The results of his continuing investigation in the areas of culture and history were published in his brilliant but fragmentary prose work *Guide to Kulchur* (1938).

Following the Great Depression of the 1930s, he turned more and more to history, especially economic history, a subject in which he had been interested since his meeting in London in 1918 with Clifford Douglas, the founder of Social Credit, an economic theory stating that maldistribution of wealth due to insufficient purchasing power is the cause of economic depressions. Pound had come to believe that a misunderstanding of money and banking by governments and the public, as well as the manipulation of money by international bankers, had led the world into a long series of wars. He became obsessed with monetary reform (*ABC of Economics*, 1933; *Social Credit*, 1935; *What Is Money For?*, 1939), involved himself in politics, and declared his admiration for the Italian dictator Benito Mussolini (*Jefferson and/or Mussolini*, 1935). The obsession affected his *Cantos*, which even earlier had shown evidence of becoming an uncontrolled series of personal and historical episodes.

ANTI-AMERICAN BROADCASTS

As war in Europe drew near, Pound returned home (1939) in the hope that he could help keep the peace between Italy and the United States. He went back to Italy a disappointed man, and between 1941 and 1943, after Italy and the United States were at war, he made several hundred broadcasts over Rome Radio on subjects ranging from James Joyce to the control of money and the U.S. government by Jewish bankers and often openly condemned the American war effort. He was arrested by U.S. forces in 1945 and spent six months in a prison camp for army criminals near Pisa. Despite harsh conditions there, he translated Confucius into English (*The Great Digest & Unwobbling Pivot*, 1951) and wrote *The Pisan Cantos* (1948), the most moving section of his long poem-in-progress.

Returned to the United States to face trial for treason, he was pronounced "insane and mentally unfit for trial" by a panel of doctors and spent 12 years (1946–58) in Saint Elizabeth's Hospital for the criminally insane in Washington, D.C. During this time he continued to write *The Cantos* (*Section: Rock-Drill*, 1955; *Thrones*, 1959), translated ancient Chinese poetry (*The Classic Anthology*, 1954) and Sophocles' *Trachiniai* (*Women of Trachis*, 1956), received visitors regularly, and kept up a voluminous and worldwide correspondence. Controversy surrounding him burst out anew when, in 1949, he was awarded the important Bollingen Prize for his *Pisan Cantos*. When on April 18, 1958, he was declared unfit to stand trial and the charges against him were dropped, he was released from Saint Elizabeth's. He returned to Italy, dividing the year between Rapallo and Venice.

Pound lapsed into silence in 1960, leaving *The Cantos* unfinished. More than 800 pages long, they are fragmentary and formless despite recurring themes and ideas. *The Cantos* are the logbook of Pound's own private voyage through Greek mythology, ancient China and Egypt, Byzantium, Renaissance Italy, the works of John Adams and Thomas Jefferson, and many other periods and subjects, including economics and banking and the nooks and crannies of his own memory and experience. Pound even convinced himself that the poem's faults and weaknesses, inevitable from the nature of the undertaking, were part of an underlying method. Yet there are numerous passages such as only he could have written that are among the best of the century.

Pound died in Venice in 1972. Out of his 60 years of publishing activity came 70 books of his own, contributions to about 70 others, and more than 1,500 articles. A complete listing of his works is in Donald Gallup, *A Bibliography of Ezra Pound* (1963; rev. ed 1983). Most of the writing on which Pound's fame now rests may be found in *Personae* (*The Collected Poems*; 1926, rev. ed. 1990), a selection of poems Pound wished to keep in print in 1926, with a few earlier and later poems added in 1949; *The Cantos* (1970), cantos 1–117, a collection of all the segments published to date; *The Spirit of Romance* (1910); *Literary Essays* (1954), the bulk of his best criticism, ed. with an introduction by T.S. Eliot; *Guide to Kulchur* (1938); and *The Letters of Ezra Pound, 1907–1941*, ed. by D.D. Paige (1950), an excellent introduction to Pound's literary life and inimitable epistolary style.

Hilda Doolittle

(b. Sept. 10, 1886, Bethlehem, Pa., U.S.—d. Sept. 27, 1961, Zürich, Switzerland)

Hilda Doolittle was an American poet, known initially as an Imagist. She was also a translator, novelist-playwright, and self-proclaimed "pagan mystic."

Doolittle's father was an astronomer, and her mother was a pianist. She was reared in the strict Moravian tradition of her mother's family. From her parents she gained, on her father's side, an intellectual inheritance, and, on her mother's, an artistic and mystical one. (The Moravians, descended in part from the German Pietists, stressed spirituality and belief in God's grace.) She entered Bryn Mawr College in 1904 and, while a student there, formed friendships with Marianne Moore, a fellow student, as well as with Ezra Pound (to whom she was briefly engaged) and William Carlos Williams, who were at the nearby University of Pennsylvania.

Ill health forced her to leave college in 1906. Five years later she traveled to Europe for what was to have been a vacation but became a permanent stay, mainly in England and Switzerland. Her first published poems, sent to *Poetry* magazine by Pound, appeared under the initials H.D., which remained thereafter her nom de plume. Other poems appeared in Pound's anthology *Des Imagistes* (1914) and in the London journal the *Egoist*, edited by Richard Aldington, to whom she was married from 1913 to 1938. Doolittle was closely associated for much of her adult life with the British novelist Bryher.

H.D.'s first volume of verse, *Sea Garden* (1916), established her as an important voice among the radical young Imagist poets. Her subsequent volumes included *Hymen* (1921), *Heliodora and Other Poems* (1924), *Red Roses for Bronze* (1931), and a trilogy comprising *The Walls Do Not Fall* (1944), *Tribute to the Angels* (1945), and *Flowering of the Rod* (1946).

The *Collected Poems of H.D.* (1925 and 1940), *Selected Poems of H.D.* (1957), and *Collected Poems 1912–1944* (1983) secured her position as a major 20th-century poet. She won additional acclaim for her translations (*Choruses from the Iphigeneia in Aulis and the Hippolytus of Euripides* [1919] and *Euripides' Ion* [1937]), for her verse drama (*Hippolytus Temporizes* [1927]), and for prose works such as *Palimpsest* (1926), *Hedylus* (1928), and, posthumously, *The Gift* (1982). Several of her books are autobiographical—including *Tribute to Freud* (1956); *Bid Me to Live* (1960); and the posthumously published *End to Torment* (1979), a memoir of Pound, and *Hermione* (1981), a semiautobiographical bildungsroman, or perhaps more accurately a *Künstlerroman* (portrait of the artist's development). *Helen in Egypt* (1961), a volume of verse, appeared shortly after her death.

Over the years H.D.'s sharp, spare, classical, and rather passionless style took on rich mythological and mystic overtones. Analyzed by Sigmund Freud, she was preoccupied with the interior journey. She was directly concerned with the woman's role as artist, and she used myth not only to illuminate individual, personal experience but also, it has been pointed out, to reconstruct a mythic past for women. H.D. is sometimes considered first among the Imagists, the seminal 20th-century poetic movement in the United States, though her work goes far beyond Imagism. She also helped define what came to be called free verse and was among the early users of a stream-of-consciousness narrative. Ezra Pound and other important 20th-century poets considered themselves artistically indebted to her.

T.S. ELIOT

(b. Sept. 26, 1888, St. Louis, Mo., U.S.—d. Jan. 4, 1965, London, Eng.)

One of the most influential authors of the 20th century, T.S. Eliot was an American-English poet, playwright, literary critic, and editor, as well as a leader of the modernist movement in poetry in such works as *The Waste Land* (1922) and *Four Quartets* (1943). His experiments in diction, style, and versification revitalized English poetry, and in a series of critical essays he shattered old orthodoxies and erected new ones. The publication of *Four Quartets* led to his recognition as the greatest living English poet and man of letters, and in 1948 he was awarded both the Order of Merit and the Nobel Prize for Literature.

EARLY YEARS

Thomas Stearns Eliot was descended from a distinguished New England family that had relocated to St. Louis, Missouri. His family allowed him the widest education available in his time, with no influence from his father to be "practical" and to go into business. From Smith Academy in St. Louis he went to Milton, in Massachusetts; from Milton he entered Harvard in 1906; he received a B.A. in 1909, after three instead of the usual four years. The men who influenced him at Harvard were George Santayana, the philosopher and poet, and the critic Irving Babbitt. From Babbitt he derived an anti-Romantic attitude that, amplified by his later reading of British philosophers F.H. Bradley and T.E. Hulme, lasted through his life. In the academic year 1909–10 he was an assistant in philosophy at Harvard.

He spent the year 1910–11 in France, attending Henri Bergson's lectures in philosophy at the Sorbonne and reading poetry with Alain-Fournier. Eliot's study of the poetry of Dante, of the English writers John Webster and John Donne, and of the French Symbolist Jules Laforgue helped him to find his own style. From 1911 to 1914 he was back at Harvard reading Indian philosophy and studying Sanskrit. In 1913 he read Bradley's *Appearance and Reality*; by 1916 he had finished, in Europe, a dissertation entitled "Knowledge and Experience in the Philosophy of F.H. Bradley." But World War I had intervened, and he never returned to Harvard

T.S. Eliot, at a reading in 1942. Poems such as The Waste Land *and "The Love Song of J. Alfred Prufrock" established Eliot as a leader in the era's modernist movement.* Kurt Hutton/Hulton Archive/Getty Images

to take the final oral examination for the Ph.D. degree. In 1914 Eliot met and began a close association with the American poet Ezra Pound.

EARLY PUBLICATIONS

Eliot was to pursue four careers: editor, dramatist, literary critic, and philosophical poet. He was probably the most erudite poet of his time in the English language. His undergraduate poems were "literary" and conventional. His first important publication, and the first masterpiece of "modernism" in English, was "The Love Song of J. Alfred Prufrock."

> *Let us go then, you and I,*
> *When the evening is spread out against the sky*
> *Like a patient etherized upon a table. . . .*

Although Pound had printed privately a small book, *A lume spento*, as early as 1908, "Prufrock" was the first poem by either of these literary revolutionists to go beyond experiment to achieve perfection. It represented a break with the immediate past as radical as that of Samuel Taylor Coleridge and William Wordsworth in *Lyrical Ballads* (1798). From the appearance of Eliot's first volume, *Prufrock and Other Observations*, in 1917, one may conveniently date the maturity of the 20th-century poetic revolution. The significance of the revolution is still disputed, but the striking similarity to the Romantic revolution of Coleridge and Wordsworth is obvious: Eliot and Pound, like their 18th-century counterparts, set about reforming poetic diction. Whereas Wordsworth thought he was going back to the "real language of men," Eliot struggled to create new verse rhythms based on the rhythms of contemporary speech. He sought a poetic diction that might be spoken by an educated person, being "neither pedantic nor vulgar."

For a year Eliot taught French and Latin at the Highgate School; in 1917 he began his brief career as a bank clerk in Lloyds Bank Ltd. Meanwhile he was also a prolific reviewer and essayist in both literary criticism and technical philosophy. In 1919 he published *Poems*, which contained the poem "Gerontion," a meditative interior monologue in blank verse: nothing like this poem had appeared in English.

THE WASTE LAND AND CRITICISM

With the publication in 1922 of his poem *The Waste Land*, Eliot won an international reputation. *The Waste Land* expresses with great power the disenchantment, disillusionment, and disgust of the period after World War I. In a series of vignettes, loosely linked by the legend of the search for the Grail, it portrays a sterile world of panicky fears and barren lusts, and of human beings waiting for some sign or promise of redemption. The poem's style is highly complex, erudite, and allusive, and the poet provided notes and references to explain the work's many quotations and allusions. This scholarly supplement distracted some readers and critics from perceiving the true originality of the poem, which lay rather in its rendering of the universal human predicament of man desiring salvation, and in its manipulation of language, than in its range of literary references. In his earlier poems Eliot had shown himself to be a master of the poetic phrase. *The Waste Land* showed him to be, in addition, a metrist of great virtuosity, capable of astonishing modulations ranging from the sublime to the conversational.

The Waste Land consists of five sections and proceeds on a principle of "rhetorical discontinuity" that reflects the fragmented experience of the 20th-century sensibility of the great modern cities of the West. Eliot expresses the hopelessness and confusion of purpose of life in the secularized city, the decay of *urbs aeterna* (the "eternal city"). This is the ultimate theme of *The Waste Land*, concretized by the poem's constant rhetorical shifts and its juxtapositions of contrasting styles. But *The Waste Land* is not a simple contrast of the heroic past with the degraded present; it is rather a timeless, simultaneous awareness of moral grandeur and moral evil. The poem's original manuscript of about 800 lines was cut down to 433 at the suggestion of Ezra Pound. *The Waste Land* is not Eliot's greatest poem, though it is his most famous.

Eliot said that the poet-critic must write "programmatic criticism"—that is, criticism that expresses the poet's own interests as a poet, quite different from historical scholarship, which stops at placing the poet in his background. Consciously intended or not, Eliot's criticism created an atmosphere in which his own poetry could be better understood and appreciated than if it had to appear in a literary milieu dominated by the standards of the preceding age. In the essay "Tradition and the Individual Talent," appearing in his first critical volume, *The Sacred Wood* (1920), Eliot asserts that tradition, as used by the poet, is not a mere repetition of the work of the immediate past ("novelty is better than repetition," he said); rather, it comprises the whole of European literature from Homer to the present. The poet writing in English may therefore make his own tradition by using materials from any past period, in any language. This point of view is "programmatic" in the sense that it disposes the reader to accept the revolutionary novelty of Eliot's polyglot quotations and serious parodies of other poets' styles in *The Waste Land*.

Also in *The Sacred Wood*, "Hamlet and His Problems" sets forth Eliot's theory of the objective correlative:

> *The only way of expressing emotion in the form of art is by finding an "objective correlative"; in other words, a set of objects, a situation, a chain of events which shall be the formula for that particular emotion; such that, when the external facts, which must terminate in sensory experience, are given, the emotion is immediately evoked.*

Eliot used the phrase "objective correlative" in the context of his own impersonal theory of poetry; it thus had an immense influence toward correcting the vagueness of late Victorian rhetoric by insisting on a correspondence of word and object. Two other essays, first published the year after *The Sacred Wood*, almost complete the Eliot critical canon: "The Metaphysical Poets" and "Andrew Marvell," published in *Selected Essays, 1917–32* (1932). In these essays he effects a new historical perspective on the hierarchy of English poetry, putting at the top Donne and other Metaphysical poets of the 17th century and lowering poets of the 18th and 19th centuries. Eliot's second famous phrase appears here — "dissociation of sensibility," invented to explain the change that came over English poetry after Donne and Andrew Marvell. This change seems to him to consist in a loss of the union of thought and feeling. The phrase has been attacked, yet the historical fact that gave rise to it cannot be denied, and with the poetry of Eliot and Pound it had a strong influence in reviving interest in certain 17th-century poets.

The first, or programmatic, phase of Eliot's criticism ended with *The Use of Poetry and the Use of Criticism* (1933) — his Charles Eliot Norton lectures at Harvard. Shortly before this his interests had broadened into theology and sociology; three short books, or long essays, were the result: *Thoughts After Lambeth* (1931), *The Idea of a Christian Society* (1939), and *Notes Towards the Definition of Culture* (1948). These book-essays, along with his *Dante* (1929), an indubitable masterpiece, broadened the base of literature into theology and philosophy: whether a work is poetry must be decided by literary standards; whether it is great poetry must be decided by standards higher than the literary.

Eliot's criticism and poetry are so interwoven that it is difficult to discuss them separately. The great essay on Dante appeared two years after Eliot was confirmed in the Church of England (1927); in that year he also became a British subject. The first long poem after his conversion was *Ash Wednesday* (1930), a religious meditation in a style entirely different from that of any of the earlier poems. *Ash Wednesday* expresses the pangs and the strain involved in the acceptance of religious belief and religious discipline. This and subsequent poems were written in a more relaxed, musical, and meditative style than his earlier works, in which the dramatic element had been stronger than the lyrical. *Ash Wednesday* was not well received in an era that held that poetry, though autonomous, is strictly secular in its outlook; it was misinterpreted by some critics as an expression of personal disillusion.

LATER POETRY AND PLAYS

Eliot's masterpiece is *Four Quartets*, which was issued as a book in 1943, though each "quartet" is a complete poem. The first of the quartets, "Burnt Norton," had appeared in the *Collected Poems* of 1936. It is a subtle meditation on the nature of time and its relation to eternity. On the model of this Eliot wrote three more poems, "East Coker" (1940), "The Dry Salvages" (1941), and "Little Gidding" (1942), in which he explored through images of great beauty and haunting power his own past, the past of the human race, and the meaning of human history. Each of the poems was self-subsistent; but when published together they were seen to make up a single work, in which themes and images recurred and were developed in a musical manner and brought to a final resolution. This work made a deep impression on the reading public, and even those who were unable to accept the poems' Christian beliefs recognized the intellectual integrity with which Eliot pursued his high theme, the originality of the form he had devised, and the technical mastery of his verse. This work led to the award to Eliot, in 1948, of the Nobel Prize for Literature.

An outstanding example of Eliot's verse in *Four Quartets* is the passage in "Little Gidding" in which the poet meets a "compound ghost," a figure composite of two of his masters: William Butler Yeats and Stéphane Mallarmé. The scene takes place at dawn in London after a night on duty at an air-raid post during an air-attack; the master speaks in conclusion:

From wrong to wrong the exasperated spirit
Proceeds, unless restored by that refining fire
Where you must move in measure, like a dancer.
The day was breaking. In the disfigured street
He left me, with a kind of valediction,
And faded on the blowing of the horn.

The passage is 72 lines, in modified terza rima; the diction is as near to that of Dante as is possible in English; and it is a fine example of Eliot's belief that a poet can be entirely original when he is closest to his models.

Eliot's plays, which begin with *Sweeney Agonistes* (published 1926; first performed in 1934) and end with *The Elder Statesman* (first performed 1958; published 1959), are, with the exception of *Murder in the Cathedral* (published and performed 1935), inferior to the lyric and meditative poetry. Eliot's belief that even secular drama attracts people who unconsciously seek a religion led him to put drama above all other forms of poetry. All his plays are in a blank verse of his own invention, in which the metrical effect is not apprehended apart from the sense; thus he brought "poetic drama" back to the popular stage. *The Family Reunion* (1939) and *Murder in the Cathedral* are Christian tragedies, the former a tragedy of revenge, the latter of the sin of pride. *Murder in the Cathedral* is a modern miracle play on the martyrdom of Thomas Becket. The most striking feature of this, his most successful play, was the use of a chorus in the traditional Greek manner to make apprehensible to common humanity the meaning of the heroic action. *The Family Reunion* (1939) was less popular. It contained scenes of great poignancy and some of the finest dramatic verse since the Elizabethans; but the public found this translation of the story of Orestes into a modern domestic drama baffling and was uneasy at the mixture of psychological realism, mythical apparitions at a drawing-room window, and a comic chorus of uncles and aunts.

After World War II, Eliot returned to writing plays with *The Cocktail Party* in 1949, *The Confidential Clerk* in 1953, and *The Elder Statesman* in 1958. These plays are comedies in which the plots are derived from Greek drama. In them Eliot accepted current theatrical conventions at their most conventional, subduing his style to a conversational level and eschewing the lyrical passages that gave beauty to his earlier plays. Only *The Cocktail Party*, which is based upon the *Alcestis* of Euripides, achieved a popular success. In spite of their obvious theatrical defects and a failure to engage the sympathies of the audience for the characters, these plays succeed in handling moral and religious issues of some complexity while entertaining the audience with farcical plots and some shrewd social satire.

Eliot's career as editor was ancillary to his main interests, but his quarterly review, *The Criterion* (1922–39), was the most distinguished international critical journal of the period. He was a "director," or working editor, of the publishing firm of Faber & Faber Ltd. from the early 1920s until his death, and as such was a generous and discriminating patron of young poets. Eliot rigorously kept his private life in the background. In 1915 he married Vivien Haigh-Wood. After 1933 she was mentally ill, and they lived apart; she died in 1947. In January 1957 he married Valerie Fletcher, with whom he lived happily until his death.

From the 1920s onward, Eliot's influence as a poet and as a critic—in both Great Britain and the United States— was immense, not least among those establishing the study of English literature as an autonomous academic discipline. He also had his detractors, ranging from avant-garde American poets who believed that he had abandoned the attempt to write about contemporary America to traditional English poets who maintained that he had broken the links between poetry and a large popular audience. During his lifetime, however, his work was the subject of much sympathetic exegesis. Since his death (and coinciding with a wider challenge to the academic study of English literature that his critical precepts did much to establish) interpreters have been markedly more critical, focusing on his complex relationship to his American origins, his elitist cultural and social views, and his exclusivist notions of tradition and of race. Nevertheless, Eliot was unequaled by any other 20th-century poet in the ways in which he commanded the attention of his audience.

WALLACE STEVENS

(b. Oct. 2, 1879, Reading, Pa., U.S.—d. Aug. 2, 1955, Hartford, Conn.)

Wallace Stevens was an American poet whose work explores the interaction of reality and what man can make of reality in his mind. It was not until late in life that Stevens was read at all widely or recognized as a major poet by more than a few.

Stevens attended Harvard for three years, worked briefly for the New York *Herald Tribune,* and then won a degree (1904) at the New York Law School and practiced law in New York City. His first published poems, aside from college verse, appeared in 1914 in *Poetry,* and thereafter he was a frequent contributor to the literary magazines. In 1916 he joined an insurance firm in Hartford, Conn., rising in 1934 to vice president, a position he held until his death.

Harmonium (1923), his first book, sold fewer than 100 copies but received some favourable critical notices; it was reissued in 1931 and in 1947. In it he introduced the imagination–reality theme that occupied his creative lifetime, making his work so unified that he considered three decades later calling his collected poems "The Whole of Harmonium."

He displayed his most dazzling verbal brilliance in his first book; he later tended to relinquish surface lustre for philosophical rigour. In *Harmonium* appeared such poems as "Le Monocle de Mon Oncle," "Sunday Morning," "Peter Quince at the Clavier," and Stevens's own favourites, "Domination of Black" and "The Emperor of Ice-Cream"; all were frequently republished in anthologies. *Harmonium* also contained "Sea Surface Full of Clouds," in which waves are described in terms of such unlikely equivalents as umbrellas, French phrases, and varieties of chocolate, and "The Comedian as the Letter C," in which he examines the relation of the poet, or man of imagination, to society.

In the 1930s and early '40s, this theme was to reappear, although not to the exclusion of others, in Stevens's *Ideas of Order* (1935), *The Man with the Blue Guitar* (1937), and *Parts of a World* (1942). *Transport to Summer* (1947) incorporated two long sequences that had appeared earlier: "Notes Towards a Supreme Fiction" and "Esthétique du Mal" ("Aesthetic of Evil"), in which he argues that beauty is inextricably linked with evil. *The Auroras of Autumn* (1950) was followed by his *Collected Poems* (1954), which earned him the Pulitzer Prize for Poetry. A volume of critical essays, *The Necessary Angel,* appeared in 1951.

After Stevens's death, Samuel French Morse edited *Opus Posthumous* (1957), including poems, plays, and prose omitted from the earlier collection.

WILLIAM CARLOS WILLIAMS

(b. Sept. 17, 1883, Rutherford, N.J., U.S. — d. March 4, 1963, Rutherford)

William Carlos Williams was an American poet who succeeded in making the ordinary appear extraordinary through the clarity and discreteness of his imagery.

After receiving an M.D. from the University of Pennsylvania in 1906 and after internship in New York and graduate study in pediatrics in Leipzig, Williams returned in 1910 to a lifetime of poetry and medical practice in his hometown.

In *Al Que Quiere!* (1917; "To Him Who Wants It!") his style was distinctly his own. Characteristic poems that proffer Williams's fresh, direct impression of the sensuous world are the frequently anthologized "Lighthearted William," "By the Road to the Contagious Hospital," and "Red Wheelbarrow."

In the 1930s during the Depression, his images became less a celebration of the world and more a catalog of its wrongs. Such poems as "Proletarian Portrait" and "The Yachts" reveal his skill in conveying attitudes by presentation rather than explanation.

In *Paterson* (5 vol., 1946–58), Williams expressed the idea of the city, which in its complexity also represents man in his complexity. The poem is based on the industrial city in New Jersey on the Passaic River and evokes a complex vision of America and modern man.

A prolific writer of prose, Williams's *In the American Grain* (1925) analyzed the American character and culture through essays on historical figures. Three novels form a trilogy about a family—*White Mule* (1937), *In the Money* (1940), and *The Build-Up* (1952). Among his notable short stories are "Jean Beicke," "A Face of Stone," and "The Farmers' Daughters." His play *A Dream of Love* (published 1948) was produced in off-Broadway and academic theatres. Williams's *Autobiography* appeared in 1951, and in 1963 he was posthumously awarded the Pulitzer Prize in poetry for his *Pictures from Brueghel, and Other Poems* (1962).

LITERARY CRITICISM

Some historians, looking back over the first half of the 20th century, were inclined to think that it was particularly noteworthy for its literary criticism. Beyond doubt, criticism thrived as it had not for several generations. It was an important influence on literature itself, and it shaped the perceptions of readers in the face of difficult new writing.

The period began with a battle between two literary groups, one that called its movement New Humanism and stood for older values in judging literature and another group that urged that old standards be overthrown and new ones adopted. The New Humanists, such as Irving Babbitt, a Harvard University professor, and Paul Elmer More, were moralists whose work found an echo in neo-traditionalist writers such as T.S. Eliot, who shared their dislike of naturalism, Romanticism, and the liberal faith in progress. The leader of the opposition, hardly a liberal himself, was the pugnacious H.L. Mencken, who insisted that the duty of writers was to present "the unvarnished truth" about life. His magazine articles and reviews gathered in *A Book of Prefaces* (1917) and the six volumes of *Prejudices* (1919–27) ushered in the iconoclasm of the 1920s, preparing the ground for satiric writers such as Sinclair Lewis. Mencken was a tireless enthusiast for the work of Joseph Conrad and Theodore Dreiser, among other modern writers. With his dislike of cant and hypocrisy, Mencken helped liberate American literature from its moralistic framework.

In this period of social change, it was natural for critics to consider literature in relationship to society and politics, as most 19th-century critics had done. The work of Van Wyck Brooks and Vernon L. Parrington illustrated two of the main approaches. In *America's Coming-of-Age* (1915), *Letters and Leadership* (1918), and *The Ordeal of Mark Twain* (1920), Brooks scolded the American public and attacked the philistinism, materialism, and provinciality of the Gilded Age. But he retreated from his critical position in the popular *Makers and Finders* series, which included *The Flowering of New England* (1936), *New England: Indian Summer* (1940), *The World of Washington Irving* (1944), *The Times of Melville and Whitman* (1947), and *The Confident Years* (1952). These books wove an elaborate cultural tapestry of the major and minor figures in American literature. In *Main Currents in American Thought* (1927–30),

Parrington, a progressive, reevaluated American literature in terms of its adherence to the tenets of Jeffersonian democracy.

The growth of Marxian influence upon thinking in the 1920s and '30s manifested itself in several critical works by V.F. Calverton, Granville Hicks, Malcolm Cowley, and Bernard Smith, as well as numerous articles in journals such as *Modern Quarterly*, *New Masses*, *Partisan Review*, and *The New Republic*. Though the enthusiasm for communism waned, Marxism contributed to the historical approach of outstanding critics such as Edmund Wilson and Kenneth Burke and to the entire school of New York intellectuals that formed around *Partisan Review* and included critics such as Lionel Trilling and Philip Rahv.

Wilson and Burke, like Cowley, Morton D. Zabel, Newton Arvin, and F.O. Matthiessen, tried to strike a balance between aesthetic concerns and social or moral issues. They were interested both in analyzing and in evaluating literary creations—i.e., they were eager to see in detail how a literary work was constructed yet also to place it in a larger social or moral framework. Their work, like that of all critics of the period, showed the influence of T.S. Eliot. In essays and books such as *The Sacred Wood* (1920) and *The Use of Poetry and the Use of Criticism* (1933), Eliot drew close attention to the language of literature yet also made sweeping judgments and large cultural generalizations. His main impact was on close readers of poetry—e.g., I.A. Richards, William Empson, and F.R. Leavis in England and the critics of the New Criticism movement in the United States, many of whom were also poets besides being political and cultural conservatives. Along with Eliot, they rewrote the map of literary history, challenged the dominance of Romantic forms and styles, promoted and analyzed difficult Modernist writing, and greatly advanced ways of discussing literary structure. Major examples of their style of close reading can be found in R.P. Blackmur's *The Double Agent* (1935), Allen Tate's *Reactionary Essays on Poetry and Ideas* (1936), John Crowe Ransom's *The World's Body* (1938), Yvor Winters's *Maule's Curse* (1938), and Cleanth Brooks's *The Well Wrought Urn* (1947). Though they were later attacked for their formalism and for avoiding the social context of writing, the New Critics did much to further the understanding and appreciation of literature.

EDMUND WILSON

(b. May 8, 1895, Red Bank, N.J., U.S.—d. June 12, 1972, Talcottville, N.Y.)

The American critic and essayist Edmund "Bunny" Wilson is recognized as one of the leading literary journalists of his time.

Educated at Princeton, Wilson moved from newspaper reporting in New York to become managing editor of *Vanity Fair* (1920–21), associate editor of *The New Republic* (1926–31), and principal book reviewer for *The New Yorker* (1944–48). Wilson's first critical work, *Axel's Castle* (1931), was an important international survey of the Symbolist tradition, in which he both criticized and praised the aestheticism of such writers as William Butler Yeats, Paul Valéry, T.S Eliot, Marcel Proust, James Joyce, and Gertrude Stein. During this period, Wilson was married for a time to writer Mary McCarthy. His next major book, *To the Finland Station* (1940), was a historical study of the thinkers who laid the groundwork for socialism and the Russian Revolution of 1917.

Much of these two books originally appeared in the pages of *The New Republic*. Until late in 1940 he was a contributor to that periodical, and much of his work for it was

Edmund Wilson. Encyclopædia Britannica, Inc.

collected in *Travels in Two Democracies* (1936), dialogues, essays, and a short story about the Soviet Union and the United States; *The Triple Thinkers* (1938), which dealt with writers involved in multiple meanings; *The Wound and the Bow* (1941), about art and neurosis; and *The Boys in the Back Room* (1941), a discussion of such new American novelists as John Steinbeck and James M. Cain. In addition to reviewing books for *The New Yorker* in the 1940s, Wilson also contributed major articles to the magazine until the year of his death, including serialization of *Upstate: Records and Recollections of Northern New York* (1972), a collection from his journals.

After World War II Wilson wrote *The Scrolls from the Dead Sea* (1955), for which he learned to read Hebrew; *Red, Black, Blond, and Olive: Studies in Four Civilizations: Zuni, Haiti, Soviet Russia, Israel* (1956); *Apologies to the Iroquois* (1960); *Patriotic Gore* (1962), an analysis of American Civil War literature; and *O Canada: An American's Notes on Canadian Culture* (1965). In this period five volumes of his magazine pieces were collected: *Europe Without Baedeker* (1947), *Classics and Commercials* (1950), *The Shores of Light* (1952), *The American Earthquake* (1958), and *The Bit Between My Teeth* (1965).

In other works Wilson gave evidence of his crotchety character: *A Piece of My Mind: Reflections at Sixty* (1956), *The Cold War and the Income Tax* (1963), and *The Fruits of the MLA* (1968), a lengthy attack on the Modern Language Association's editions of American authors, which he felt buried their subjects in pedantry. His plays are in part collected in *Five Plays* (1954) and in *The Duke of Palermo and Other Plays with an Open Letter to Mike Nichols* (1969). His poems appear in *Notebooks of Night* (1942) and in *Night Thoughts* (1961); an early collection, *Poets, Farewell*, appeared in 1929. *Memoirs of Hecate County* (1946) is a collection of short stories that encountered censorship problems when it first appeared. Wilson edited the posthumous papers and notebooks of his college friend F. Scott Fitzgerald, *The Crack-Up* (1945), and also edited the novel *The Last Tycoon* (1941), which Fitzgerald had left uncompleted at his death. Wilson wrote one novel himself, *I Thought of Daisy* (1929). *The Twenties: From Notebooks and Diaries of the Period*, edited by Leon Edel, was published posthumously in 1975. His widow, Elena, edited *Letters on Literature and Politics 1912–1972* (1977), and his correspondence with the novelist Vladimir Nabokov appeared in 1979 (revised and expanded edition *Dear Bunny, Dear Volodya: The Nabokov-Wilson Letters, 1940–1971*, 2001).

Wilson concerned himself with both literary and social themes and wrote as historian, poet, novelist, editor, and short-story writer. Unlike some of his contemporaries, such as the New Critics, Wilson thought that a text or topic could be best examined by placing it at the centre of intersecting ideas and contexts, whether biographical, political, social, linguistic, or philosophical. He covered a multitude of subjects, probing each with an expansiveness that was firmly rooted in scholarship and common sense, and he expressed his views in a prose style noted for its clarity and precision. His critical writings on the American novelists Ernest Hemingway, John Dos Passos, F. Scott Fitzgerald, and William Faulkner attracted public interest to their early work and guided opinion toward their acceptance.

KENNETH BURKE

(b. May 5, 1897, Pittsburgh, Pa., U.S.—d. Nov. 19, 1993, Andover, N.J.)

The literary critic Kenneth Burke is best known for his rhetorically based analyses of the nature of knowledge and for his views of literature as "symbolic action," where language and human agency combine.

Burke attended universities briefly—Ohio State University (Columbus, 1916–17) and Columbia University (New York City, 1917–18)—but never took a degree. He wrote poems, a novel, and short stories and translated the works of many German writers into English. He was the music critic of *The Dial* (1927–29) and of *The Nation* (1934–36). He then turned to literary criticism, lecturing on this subject at the University of Chicago (1938; 1949–50), and he taught at Bennington College (Vermont) from 1943 through 1961.

Burke's unorthodox critical thought is complex and subtle. He was concerned not to look only at the "intrinsic" elements of literature (the formal aspects of the literary text itself), and he called for a larger view that also included a work's "extrinsic" elements—the relationship of the literary work to its full context (its audience, its author's biography, its social, historical, and political background). Realizing that the critic should criticize criticism as well as literature, he became an early advocate for literary theory. Among his books are: *Counter-Statement* (1931;

New Criticism

New Criticism was a post–World War I school of Anglo-American literary critical theory that insisted on the intrinsic value of a work of art and focused attention on the individual work alone as an independent unit of meaning. It was opposed to the critical practice of bringing historical or biographical data to bear on the interpretation of a work.

The primary technique employed in the New Critical approach is close, analytic reading of the text, a technique as old as Aristotle's *Poetics*. The New Critics, however, introduced refinements into the method. Early seminal works in the tradition were those of the English critics I.A. Richards (*The Principles of Literary Criticism*, 1924) and William Empson (*Seven Types of Ambiguity*, 1930). The movement did not have a name, however, until the appearance of John Crowe Ransom's *The New Criticism* (1941), a work that loosely organized the principles of this basically linguistic approach to literature. Some figures associated with New Criticism include Cleanth Brooks, R.P. Blackmur, and W.K. Wimsatt, Jr., although their critical pronouncements, along with those of Ransom, Richards, and Empson, are somewhat diverse and do not readily constitute a uniform school of thought. New Criticism was eclipsed as the dominant mode of Anglo-American literary criticism by the 1970s.

To the New Critics, poetry was a special kind of discourse, a means of communicating feeling and thought that could not be expressed in any other kind of language. It differed qualitatively from the language of science or philosophy, but it conveyed equally valid meanings. Such critics set out to define and formalize the qualities of poetic thought and language, utilizing the technique of close reading with special emphasis on the connotative and associative values of words and on the multiple functions of figurative language—symbol, metaphor, and image—in the work. Poetic form and content could not be separated, since the experience of reading the particular words of a poem, including its unresolved tensions, is the poem's "meaning."

rev. ed., 1968); *The Philosophy of Literary Form* (1941; 3rd ed., 1974); *Permanence and Change: An Anatomy of Purpose* (1935; rev. ed., 1959); *Attitudes Toward History*, 2 vol. (1937; rev. ed., 1959); *A Grammar of Motives* (1945); *A Rhetoric of Motives* (1950); and *Language as Symbolic Action* (1966).

JOHN CROWE RANSOM
(b. April 30, 1888, Pulaski, Tenn., U.S. — d. July 4, 1974, Gambier, Ohio)

The poet and critic John Crowe Ransom was a leading theorist of the Southern literary renaissance that began after World War I. Ransom's *The New Criticism* (1941) provided the name of the influential mid-20th-century school of criticism.

Ransom, whose father was a minister, lived during his childhood in several towns in the Nashville, Tenn., area. He attended Vanderbilt University in Nashville for two years, then dropped out to teach because he felt his father should not continue to support him. He later returned to the university and graduated in 1909 at the head of his class. Subsequently he went to Oxford University as a Rhodes scholar. From 1914 to 1937 he taught English at Vanderbilt, where he was the leader of the Fugitives, a group of poets that published the influential literary magazine *The Fugitive* (1922–25) and shared a belief in the South and its regional traditions.

Ransom was also among those Fugitives who became known as the Agrarians. Their *I'll Take My Stand* (1930) criticized the idea that industrialization was the answer to the needs of the South.

Ransom taught from 1937 until his retirement in 1958 at Kenyon College in Gambier, Ohio, where he founded and edited (1939–59) the literary magazine *The Kenyon Review*. Ransom's literary studies include *God Without Thunder* (1930); *The World's Body* (1938), in which he takes the position that poetry and science furnish different but equally valid knowledge about the world; *Poems and Essays* (1955); and *Beating the Bushes: Selected Essays, 1941–1970* (1972). Ransom's poetry, which one critic has applauded as exhibiting weighty facts "in small or delicate settings," often deals with the subjects of self-alienation and death. His poetry is collected in *Chills and Fever* (1924) and *Two Gentlemen in Bonds* (1927). Thereafter he published only five new poems; his *Selected Poems* (1945; rev. ed., 1969), which won a National Book Award, contains revisions of his earlier work. T.D. Young edited his critical essays (1968). *Selected Essays of John Crowe Ransom* appeared in 1984.

CLEANTH BROOKS

(b. Oct. 16, 1906, Murray, Ky., U.S.—d. May 10, 1994, New Haven, Conn.)

Cleanth Brooks was an American teacher and critic whose work was important in establishing the New Criticism, which stressed close reading and structural analysis of literature.

Educated at Vanderbilt University, Nashville, Tenn., and at Tulane University, New Orleans, Brooks was a Rhodes scholar (Exeter College, Oxford) before he began teaching at Louisiana State University, Baton Rouge, in 1932. From 1935 to 1942, with Charles W. Pipkin and poet and critic Robert Penn Warren, he edited *The Southern Review*, a journal that advanced the New Criticism and published the works of a new generation of Southern writers. Brooks's critical works include *Modern Poetry and the Tradition* (1939) and *The Well Wrought Urn* (1947). Authoritative college texts by Brooks, with others, reinforced the popularity of the New Criticism: *Understanding Poetry* (1938) and *Understanding Fiction* (1943), written with Warren, and *Understanding Drama* (1945), with Robert Heilman.

Brooks taught at Yale University from 1947 to 1975 and was also a Library of Congress fellow (1951–62) and cultural attaché at the U.S. embassy in London (1964–66). Brooks's later works included *Literary Criticism: A Short History* (1957; cowritten with William K. Wimsatt); *A Shaping Joy: Studies in the Writer's Craft* (1972); *The Language of the American South* (1985); *Historical Evidence and the Reading of Seventeenth Century Poetry* (1991); and several books on William Faulkner, including *William Faulkner: The Yoknapatawpha Country* (1963), *William Faulkner: Toward Yoknapatawpha and Beyond* (1978), *William Faulkner: First Encounters* (1983), and *Firm Beliefs of William Faulkner* (1987).

EPILOGUE

Like the country itself, American literature underwent a number of drastic changes from the end of the 19th century through the first half of the 20th century. The crisis of national identity precipitated by the Civil War in the 1860s, which saw the theretofore seemingly unified American spirit abruptly divided with the secession of the Confederacy, found no resolution in the decades after the war's end. This fragmented character was then further unraveled in the works of many authors around the turn of the 20th century. As these writers lived through the radical societal and technological changes of the time, a broader variety of perspectives came about through which the concept of America was filtered.

Similarly, the literary works themselves—regardless of whether or not they touched on fundamental issues of "Americanism"—grew more diverse as new, nonrealist narrative structures came into being. The evolution of literary trends, from faithfully representative naturalism to the untethered experimentation of modernism, continued throughout the 1900s. By the century's midpoint, after the ramifications of two calamitous World Wars had begun to sink in, a new literary movement—postmodernism— came into being as a fractured America was plunged into the era of mass media, which would have revolutionary effects on the country in the latter half of the 20th century.

Algonquin Round Table The name give to an informal group of American literary men and women who met daily for lunch on weekdays at a large round table in the Algonquin Hotel in New York City during the 1920s and '30s.

bohemian A person, typically a writer or artist, who lives an unconventional life, usually in a colony with others of like mind.

chattel An item of tangible movable or immovable property except real estate and things (as buildings) connected with real property; commonly attached to livestock and, formerly, to slaves.

epigrammatic Relating to or resembling an epigram, which is a concise poem on a single theme with a turn of thought at the end.

epistolary novel A novel told through the medium of letters written by one or more of the characters.

episodic narrative A story told in a series of episodes; a serial.

imbroglio An intricate or complicated situation, often marked by a painful or embarrassing misunderstanding.

impressionistic Based on or involving impression as distinct from expertise or fact.

juvenilia Compositions produced in an author's youth.

Little Theatre movement Movement in U.S. theatre to free dramatic forms and methods of production from the limitations of the large commercial theatres by establishing small experimental centres of drama.

local colourist One who writes in a style derived from the presentation of the features and peculiarities of a particular locality and its inhabitants.

Lost Generation Specifically, a group of U.S. writers who came of age during World War I and established their literary reputations in the 1920s.

modernism In the arts, a radical break with the past and the concurrent search for new forms of expression.

muckraker Any of a group of American writers, identified with pre–World War I reform and exposé literature.

mythopoeic Of or relating to the making of myth.

naturalism A late 19th- and early 20th-century movement inspired by adaptation of the principles and methods of natural science to literature and art, especially the Darwinian view of nature.

New Criticism The post-World War I school of Anglo-American literary critical theory that insisted on the intrinsic value of a work of art and focused attention on the individual work alone as an independent unit of meaning.

posthumous Following or occurring after death.

pseudonym A fictitious name; a pen name under which an author may have written.

transcendentalism A 19th-century movement of New England writers and philosophers loosely bound together by a belief in the essential unity of all creation, the innate goodness of man, and the supremacy of insight over logic and experience for the revelation of the deepest truths.

BIBLIOGRAPHY

Literary histories and major anthologies include Robert E. Spiller et al. (eds.), *Literary History of the United States*, 4th ed., rev., 2 vol. (1974), a standard general work; Marcus Cunliffe (ed.), *American Literature to 1900*, new ed. (1986, reissued 1993), and *American Literature Since 1900*, new ed. (1987, reissued 1993); Vernon Louis Parrington, *Main Currents in American Thought: An Interpretation of American Literature from the Beginnings to 1920*, 3 vol. (1927–30, reissued 1987), essential background reading; Walter Blair et al. (eds.), *The Literature of the United States*, 3rd ed., 2 vol. (1966); Cleanth Brooks, R.W.B. Lewis, and Robert Penn Warren (compilers), *American Literature: The Makers and the Making*, 2 vol. (1973); and Alfred Kazin, *An American Procession* (1984), portraits of individual writers from Emerson to Fitzgerald. Since the 1980s, anthologies have shifted to a multicultural viewpoint with broad coverage of writing by women and minorities. The most controversial example has been Paul Lauter and Richard Yarborough (eds.), *The Heath Anthology of American Literature*, 2nd ed., 2 vol. (1994). Recent full-scale literary histories representing the work of younger scholars include Emory Elliott et al. (eds.), *The Columbia Literary History of the United States* (1991); and Sacvan Bercovitch and Cyrus R.K. Patell (eds.), *The Cambridge History of American Literature* (1994–2005). Blanche E. Gelfant (ed.), *The Columbia Companion to the Twentieth-Century American Short Story* (2000), is a comprehensive guide to short fiction.

Studies that focus on the period from the Civil War to the 20th century include: Jay Martin, *Harvests of Change:*

American Literature, 1865–1914 (1964), a comprehensive study; Arthur Hobson Quinn, *A History of the American Drama, from the Beginning to the Civil War,* 2nd ed. (1943, reprinted 1979), and *A History of the American Drama, from the Civil War to the Present Day,* rev. ed. (1964, reprinted 1980), the most thorough treatment; Alfred Kazin, *On Native Grounds: An Interpretation of Modern American Prose Literature* (1942, reprinted 1982), a brilliantly written critical history; and Morton Dauwen Zabel (ed.), *Literary Opinion in America,* 3rd ed., rev., 2 vol. (1962).

Important studies of the pastoral and frontier traditions in American literature are Henry Nash Smith, *Virgin Land: The American West as Symbol and Myth* (1950, reissued 1978); R.W.B. Lewis, *The American Adam: Innocence, Tragedy, and Tradition in the Nineteenth Century* (1955, reissued 1984); Leo Marx, *The Machine in the Garden: Technology and the Pastoral Ideal in America* (1964, reprinted 1972); and, from a radically different viewpoint, Richard Slotkin, *The Fatal Environment: The Myth of the Frontier in the Age of Industrialization, 1800–1890* (1985). Major work on the romance tradition in American fiction is developed in Richard Chase, *The American Novel and Its Tradition* (1957, reprinted 1978); and Leslie Fiedler, *Love and Death in the American Novel,* rev. ed. (1966, reissued 1992); as well as in later studies such as Joel Porte, *The Romance in America: Studies in Cooper, Poe, Hawthorne, Melville, and James* (1969); and Michael Davitt Bell, *The Development of American Romance* (1980). Other work on American realism, stressing the social and historical context, includes Eric J. Sundquist (ed.), *American Realism: New Essays* (1982); Philip Fisher, *Hard Facts: Setting and Form in the American Novel* (1985); Amy Kaplan, *The Social Construction of American Realism* (1988); and David E. Shi, *Facing Facts* (1995). The role of race in American literature is the ambitious subject of Eric J. Sundquist, *To Wake the Nations*

(1993); while ethnicity is closely analyzed in Werner Sollors, *Beyond Ethnicity: Consent and Descent in American Culture* (1986). Other influential studies include Ann Douglas, *Terrible Honesty: Mongrel Manhattan in the 1920s* (1995), focusing on race and culture; and Michael Denning, *The Cultural Front* (1996), an exploration of left-wing literary culture in the 1930s.

The wide range of neglected novels by 19th-century women has been mapped by Susan K. Harris, *19th-Century American Women's Novels* (1990). Feminist criticism of American fiction can be found in Judith Fetterley, *The Resisting Reader* (1978). Radical and ethnic writing between the two world wars has been studied by Walter B. Rideout, *The Radical Novel in the United States, 1900–1954* (1956, reissued 1992); Daniel Aaron, *Writers on the Left* (1961, reissued 1992); and Marcus Klein, *Foreigners: The Making of American Literature, 1900–1940* (1981). The long history of African American literature has been explored by Robert A. Bone, *The Negro Novel in America*, rev. ed. (1965); Robert B. Stepto, *From Behind the Veil*, 2nd ed. (1991); and Henry Louis Gates, Jr., *The Signifying Monkey* (1988). A succinct survey of Jewish American writing can be found in Allen Guttmann, *The Jewish Writer in America* (1971).

INDEX

E

F

Fable, A, 147, 150, 153
"Face of Stone, A," 218
Face of Time, The, 125
Family Reunion, 214
Farewell to Arms, A, 135, 136, 137, 138
"Farmer's Daughters, The," 218
Farrell, James T., 73, 85, 117, 124–125
"Farther in Summer than the Birds," 55
Fascism, 52, 98, 124, 195, 202
Faulkner, William, 111, 116, 133, 140–151, 224, 228
Faulkner-Cowley File, The, 148–149
"Fear of Man, The," 184
Federal Theatre Project, 124, 176
feminism, 24, 41–42, 60–61, 65, 91, 104, 108, 115, 118, 126, 129, 154
Fighting Angel, 113
Fine Clothes to the Jew, 191
"Fish, The," 194
Fitzgerald, F. Scott, 116, 117, 119–122, 134, 139, 223, 224
Flags in the Dust, 142
Flaubert, Gustave, 90, 143, 199
Flowering Judas, 154, 157
Flowering Peach, The, 175
Following the Equator, 36
Ford, Ford Madox, 84, 104, 196
Forgotten Village, 153
For Whom the Bell Tolls, 136, 137, 138
Foundry, The, 118
Four Million, 26
Four Quartets, 178, 206, 212–213
Four Saints in Three Acts, 108
Freeman, Mary E. Wilkins, 23
free verse, 177, 178, 186, 188, 200, 206
"Frenzied Finance," 53
frontier, decline of, 21, 154, 155

Frost, Robert, 176–177, 179–187, 195, 197
Fruits of the MLA, The, 223
Fugitives, 226
Further Range, A, 176, 183

G

Gale, Zona, 106
Garland, Hamlin, 69, 73, 74, 83
General William Booth Enters into Heaven, and Other Poems, 177
'Genius,' The, 77, 80
George's Mother, 85
Germinie Lacerteux, 71
"Gerontion," 209
Gift, The, 205
"Gift Outright, The," 183
Gilded Age, criticism of America during, 45–54
Gilded Age, The, 30, 45
Gladstone, William, 90
Go Down, Moses, 147
Gold, Michael, 154
Golden Bowl, The, 87, 94
Golden Boy, 175, 176
Goncourt, Edmond and Jules de, 71, 90
Good Earth, The, 113
Good Morning, America, 188
Grant, Ulysses S., 34, 47
Grapes of Wrath, The, 151, 152
Great American Fraud, 54
Great Depression, 78, 110, 116, 118, 126, 136, 148, 149, 151, 188, 202, 218
Greatest Trust in the World, The, 53
Great Gatsby, The, 116, 119, 121
Great God Brown, The, 167
Green Hills of Africa, The, 135